Alison Murdoch

BED 12

HIKARI
PRESS

First published in 2017
by Hikari Press, London

www.hikaripress.co.uk

Distributed in the UK by
Combined Book Services Limited
Paddock Wood Distribution Centre
Paddock Wood
Tonbridge
Kent TN12 6UU

ISBN: 978-0-9956478-0-0

Hikari Press gratefully acknowledges the financial support of
Arts Council England through Grants for the Arts.

British Library Cataloguing-in-Publication-Data.
A catalogue record of the book is available
from the British Library.

Designed in Albertina by Libanus Press
and printed in England by
Short Run Press

This book is dedicated to kindness: the kindness that Simon and I have received from our family, friends and spiritual teachers; the kindness of everyone at St Thomas' Hospital; and the everyday kindnesses that sustain the lives of every being on this planet.

'Whenever possible, be kind. It is always possible'

– The Dalai Lama

Acknowledgements

The names of the clinical staff at St Thomas' Hospital have been changed to protect their privacy.

Any philosophical views expressed here are merely those of the author. For a more reliable introduction to Buddhist philosophy and psychology see *The Art of Happiness: A Handbook for Living* by the Dalai Lama and Howard Cutler, and *A Fearless Heart: Why Compassion is the Key to Greater Wellbeing* by Thupten Jinpa.

Contents

Foreword

When sudden illness strikes wise, compassionate people we can only hope they find the strength to write about it. Alison Murdoch's poignant account of her husband's life-threatening encephalitis is so much more than a patient's story. It is a beautifully written reflection on the joy and fragility of life, and how any life under threat has to be lived in the moment. It is a contemplation of the inevitability of death, and why we should not shy away from accepting death while living each day as if it could be our last. Above all, it is a love letter to the NHS, and to the everyday acts of kindness that keep it afloat. 'On the other side of the Atlantic, Simon's illness probably would have bankrupted both ourselves and our families . . . At its best, the NHS is an organism that functions like the barometer of a healthy society – a gesture of collective wisdom and mutual generosity which enables us to support each other through the worst of times.'

We all fall into the river of illness eventually, and this book will be of particular comfort to anyone seeking the courage and inner strength to drag a loved one back to the bank. As one of Simon's nurses observed: "I wish everyone could have an Alison." In times of terrible stress, we learn most from those who've also been there. If you want to understand the power of compassion, why comas aren't always peaceful, and how some people recover from a near death experience and are able to laugh about it afterwards, many of the answers are in this precious gem of a book.

Dr Phil Hammond,
NHS doctor, writer, broadcaster and comedian

The heavy wooden door is designed to open inwards.

"What am I doing here?!" I ask myself, in a sudden panic.

I weigh the key in my hand, and with great resistance put it in the lock.

It turns with a quiet click, and I slowly push the door open.

Inside is a vast room, its edges lost in gloom.

In the middle of the room is a dark and silent swimming pool.

The only way in is to dive.

The water is not as cold as I expected it to be.

I start to write.

WEEK ONE
EMERGENCY

CHAPTER 1

The ambulance

It is 2.30pm on a sunny Monday afternoon in July. I wouldn't normally be at home, but I have an urgent document to write and there will be less distraction away from the office. I've been staring at a computer screen since the beginning of the day and decide to enjoy a few minutes of fresh air before making myself a late lunch. So I'm standing on our front path in South London when I suddenly look up to see my 58-year-old husband open the gate with the unsteadiness of a man in his mid-eighties. I gasp. I've never seen him look like that before. His eyes are half-closed, his skin pale and his movements painfully slow, but I can't pinpoint why he is so dramatically changed. It's just an immediate wordless knowledge that something is dreadfully wrong.

I run to open the door, and ease him onto the sofa. "What's happened?!" He is drawing short strange breaths and can only manage a few words. "Fell ill in Winchester … came back early". "Did you take a taxi from the station?" "No". "Have you had anything to drink?" "Yes". "Have you had anything to eat?" "No." I pull off his shoes and leave him there to rest, returning to the kitchen to prepare my lunch. I'm trying to keep anxiety at arm's length while I collect my thoughts. Within less than a minute it's clear that chopping salad is a ridiculous thing to be doing and that I need to get Simon into bed. So I cajole him up our two flights of stairs, standing behind him on each step in case he slips.

I only realise how serious things are when we reach the bedroom. Simon falls rigid and wordless across the bed, from left to right. When I try to undo his belt buckle, he screams. "You have to tell me what is going on and where the pain is!" I respond. Silence. I know

I'm married to a bit of a drama queen, but this is extreme. I repeat, very slowly and loudly: "Unless you speak to me I'm going to call an ambulance." Silence. It dawns on me that this is now what I am going to do. To call an ambulance for my husband feels like crossing a line, breaking a taboo.

I dash downstairs for the cordless phone, then back to the bedroom. I get through immediately, noticing how strange my voice sounds, and forcing patience at all the banal questions. The operator tells me that an ambulance is on its way, to collect together any medicines that Simon uses, and to get household pets out of the way. I look down at Simon. His cat Zampano has insinuated himself into the crook of his master's inert arm, and my cat Mina is pacing fretfully around his feet. This is a family affair, and they aren't going anywhere.

A few minutes later I hear an ambulance siren in the distance and realise with a start that this time it is for us. Our bedroom is suddenly full of uniforms and medical equipment. When Simon is asked for our address he answers with a stream of delirious nonsense. OK, so this really is serious. Putting his arms around their shoulders, the ambulance team half-carry him downstairs without even bothering to put his shoes on. Simon has aged well—his mane of curly hair now pepper-grey, his features stronger than before. In his character-istic black jeans and an open-necked white linen shirt he looks like a wounded Byronic hero. Behind them, I move quickly to scoop up the kinds of sensible items that might be needed for an overnight stay in hospital: dressing gown, reading glasses and book for Simon, and laptop and working papers for me, so that my busy schedule won't be unduly disrupted.

The inside of the ambulance is a self-sufficient and scaled-down version of a hospital workstation. We are stationary on the street outside our house, yet strangely isolated from the world outside. More tests are done, in a frustratingly measured and methodical way. The obvious diagnosis is a stroke but Simon's blood pressure is fine. After what seems like a month we're on our way. I phone the office quickly to explain that I will miss a late afternoon appointment, and ask the ambulance crew where we are going. St Thomas'. One of the best hospitals in the world—great! By now Simon is almost unconscious. I wonder why there is no siren and fret at how slowly the traffic lights change.

When we arrive at the hospital Simon is lifted into a clunky type of wheelchair that I've never seen before and we hurry into the Accident & Emergency department. He is asked to clench his hands. He clearly thinks he is doing this but nothing happens. The gravity of what is unfolding begins to sink in.

CHAPTER 2

Prelude

Where do ideas come from? Years ago I had a foreboding that one day Simon would go to work in the morning and never come back. Ever since, I've tried to be there on the doorstep to watch him head off on his bicycle and to make a wish and a prayer for his safe return.

We are both tired when the emergency happens, but that's nothing unusual. We don't have children but we each work at least six days a week running small charities, with the accompanying pressures of raising funds, supporting over-worked staff and juggling countless out-of-hours commitments. However, we're going away the following Saturday with wonderful plans for the whole of August: hosting my mother-in-law's ninetieth birthday in Devon, then flying to Galicia for a friend's wedding, followed by a lazy ten-day meander with a tent along the northern coast of Spain. From Bilbao Simon will return to work and I'll continue on to a programme of teachings by the Dalai Lama in Toulouse, followed by the first international conference organised by the charity that I work for. It's a plan that brings together all the ingredients we love—family, friends and celebration; spontaneity and fresh air; outer and inner adventure.

I've noticed before that whenever I'm about to go away life speeds up and becomes a race to get everything done, right up to the huge sigh of relief when I actually board the bus, car, train or plane. For me, the week ahead felt challenging but do-able, plotted out to the nth degree and under the strict control of lists and priorities. Simon would typically tackle his tasks in a different way. Definitely no lists, just a chaotic whole-hearted engagement with all the people and issues that come his way and a willingness to work late into the evening to do the rest.

It isn't unknown for us to stay up all night before a holiday to clear our emails. Yet whenever someone tells me that we work too hard, I respond that we relax hard as well. Our first honeymoon was to Hungary, which for a host of unfathomable reasons is Simon's favourite country. I found it such hard going that the following year I organised what became known as 'the revenge honeymoon' to my own favourite country, Tibet. "My heart yearns for a simple English country church," said Simon ungratefully, as we exited from yet another fantastically-decorated temple in which he'd watched his new wife pore over rows of statues with the distinctive smell of over-ripe butter. My mother later remarked that the fact we'd survived that trip together gave her some optimism that our marriage would also endure.

Before he met me Simon was in the habit of taking long-distance cycle trips—from Nice to Barcelona, from Bucharest to Budapest, and most memorably from Sofia to Istanbul. The last of those journeys had been interrupted by the loss of his bike, when thieves decided to saw down the tree to which it had been chained. Just before his fiftieth birthday, Simon was inspired by Satish Kumar's book *No Destination* to make a longer journey, this time on foot. He saw this as the interval between Act 1 and Act 2 of his life, and since there was nowhere he particularly wanted to walk to, he decided to walk home to me and the cats. As a lover of Hungary, his plan was simply to fly to Budapest, follow the Danube north and then turn west at Krakow.

Simon's solitary pilgrimage across some of the most historically rich landscapes of Northern Europe took three and a half months, and when we met up in Calais I hardly recognised this whippet-thin and introspective man wearing frayed and faded clothes, topped by a beard straight out of a wilderness movie. From my side, my initial admiration at the carefree romanticism of setting off without a map, sleeping rough in the woods and making a solitary crossing of the snow-bound Tatra mountains had turned to mild irritation at the hotel and opera bills that I was expected to pay as he walked his way across the Weimar Republic, paying homage at the shrines of his heroes Bach, Beethoven and Goethe.

This time, our departure on holiday was complicated by Simon having been ill the preceding weekend, with the kind of flu virus that often results from being a bit run down. On the Friday evening he'd organised the kind of romantic evening that we didn't often have time for these days. The early stages of our relationship were full of riddles and clues about where and when to meet that could easily land me inappropriately dressed and ill-equipped at the wrong end of London or even of Europe. "Lunch in an interesting city, followed by a voyage to where the mountains meet the sea" coupled with a deliberately misleading "bring your grey watercolour paints" was all the advance information I received for a surprise summer holiday in Sardinia, reached via a flight to Genoa and an overnight ferry crossing. I was glad that I'd decided to pack my bathing costume, just in case.

The invitation that previous Friday had been relatively simple: "138 Kennington Park Road, 7pm." I looked up the address online and found it to be the White Bear pub theatre not far from our house. Simon's unpunctuality is so habitual and extreme that he's jokingly known as The Late Mr Simon Keyes, but on this occasion when he turned up late and ordered a soft drink I could see he wasn't feeling well. At the interval we decided to go home and get an early night. The next day he stayed in bed while I met my mother and niece for lunch, and on the Sunday he felt so much better that we went to a matinee at the National Theatre. We both remember this being a particularly sweet and special day, as if tinged with golden light. In the evening, he cleaned the bathroom while I mowed the lawn.

On the Monday morning Simon had slept badly and was feeling off colour again. He didn't have a temperature, just aches, pains and a headache. I sat down with him on the sofa. "Don't go to work." "I have to, there's a meeting I can't miss in Winchester." "You won't achieve anything feeling like this. Can you postpone it?" "No." "Can someone else go instead?" "No." With a sigh, I gave him a tall glass of fizzy vitamin C and a bowl of muesli with yoghurt and fresh fruit, both of which he left untouched. Half an hour later I watched him disappear round the corner on his bike, noticing a bit more of a wobble than usual.

CHAPTER 3

A&E

Things go rapidly downhill as soon as we arrive at A&E. When Simon is asked to stick out his tongue, as he had done for the ambulance staff less than an hour before, he can no longer do this. Without a hint of NHS delay he is wheeled straight into a cubicle where a huddle of white-coated doctors cluster around his trolley bed. I am pleasantly surprised to find that most of the time I am allowed to listen in. Every now and again I am asked to leave and the blue curtains are drawn around the cubicle to conceal what's happening inside. These are the worst moments.

Afterwards, the doctors use euphemisms such as "agitated" and "combative". Actually, it looks and feels like something out of *The Exorcist*. Simon is now completely delirious, writhing from side to side and pulling back in agony whenever someone touches him. When the medical team try to make him swallow an aspirin he spits it across the room. At one point it takes several uniformed men to hold him down and his screams echo down the corridors. When his blood pressure drops to 60 over 40, a beeper goes off and eight people rush around the bed and slam an oxygen mask on his face. I am blessed with an almost complete lack of medical knowledge, and only find out later how serious this could have been.

Everyone is extremely kind to me, bringing me hot drinks in polystyrene cups and offering me a mobile phone should I wish to make calls from 'Room A' next door. A more seasoned hospital visitor might have taken this as a message that something particularly dramatic and worrying was going on. Sometimes I have no choice but to leave the cubicle, when the distress of seeing Simon so raw, frightened and stripped back comes close to overwhelming me.

At one point a young doctor with pale skin called Martin tells me that the results of the brain scan are OK. Oh, so he had a brain scan? It seems only five minutes later when Martin returns, apologetic and even paler, to tell me that the doctors have now identified some damage to the right front cortex. "What goes on in there?" I ask, hoping my memory is wrong. "Empathy and relationships."

For the first and only time I go outside to howl. Leaning on a grey concrete wall in the ambulance bay and looking up at the sky I'm outraged at how normal everything looks. When I've said my piece to the universe I realise I'm locked out, and have to ask one of the ambulance drivers to let me back inside.

Every now and again a consultant asks me to repeat the history of Simon's mystery illness, looking for any clues that might assist diagnosis. I have now managed to track down his colleague Laura who travelled to Winchester with him that morning. When they met at Waterloo she noticed him walking unsteadily, and on the train he complained of being shivery and having a terrible headache, and he couldn't finish his sentences. He had trouble stepping onto the platform at the other end but insisted that she continue on to their meeting. Characteristically, before they parted he rallied himself sufficiently to go through the meeting agenda with her. Five minutes later she watched him haul himself onto another train for the journey back to London, and has been beside herself with worry ever since.

By now the A&E staff are using injections to sedate my husband, and I am invited to return to the cubicle to spend a few minutes together before they put him fully under. The blue curtains are pulled around us in a gesture of privacy. I'd swear I only get 30 seconds, and as I kiss his warm face I wonder if it will soon be waxy and cold, just like my father's skin after a fatal heart attack a few years previously.

The charity that I work for is based in one of London's Tibetan Buddhist centres. In a lovely demonstration of the compassion that sits at the heart of Buddhist practice, my colleague Esther is the first person to come and find me at the hospital. She is laden with snacks, pyjamas, prayer books and a small *stupa*, a symbolic representation of the enlightened mind that is traditionally touched to the chest and head of a dying person. I put the *stupa* firmly but discreetly to one side. Esther's partner Tricia arrives to join us, bringing with her some freshly squeezed carrot and orange juice. As any sense of time or place shrinks away every small detail becomes more vivid and memorable.

Esther is surprised that I am still on my own after so many hours. With all my attention focused on Simon it hasn't crossed my mind to ask anyone else to join me. Falling back on traditional family hierarchies I start with Simon's only brother Tim, who is the headmaster of a school in Worcester and in the middle of his summer holidays. Tim is driving through a Scottish glen when he gets my call, so I ask him to pull over. He said later that he'd never heard my voice sound like that before. Tim asks whether he should drive down from Scotland. I reply: "Well, there are three possibilities: either Simon will be dead before you get here, or you'll be just in time, or he'll pull through." Afterwards, I felt bad about having been so forthright, but Tim said it was actually quite helpful.

Some time later Tim calls back a second time for news and tells me that he's decided to ring Simon's mother who is at home in Malvern, Worcestershire. It isn't a light decision given that she is 89 years old. With a weird sense of propriety I feel this gives me permission to ring my own mother in Sussex, who is also in her eighties. "Are you sitting down? I'm afraid I've got bad news."

Esther is clearly loath to leave me on my own so I rack my brains about who else I can call on. There isn't anyone obvious, because it would usually be Simon, until I remember Philip, Simon's best friend and our best man. After a bit of phone tag (he was at a concert) we manage to connect and he offers to get a taxi over to the hospital straightaway. Two other friends, Mike and Mhairi, jump in a cab the minute they get my message. Mike previously worked as a hospital porter and doesn't want me to be on my own should bad news come through—he knows at first hand what it can be like. I wonder later whether I would have had the same readiness to turn a Monday evening upside-down.

I am told that Simon is "very, very ill." When I ask one of the doctors if his life is in danger he plays with words while his body language tells me, undeniably, that yes, it is. I shut myself up in Room A and scroll down both our phones, ringing anyone we know, anywhere in the world, who might be willing to make prayers. It feels like I am in a Western with a smoking gun in each hand. If people don't respond sometimes I leave a message and sometimes not, depending on how emotionally robust I think they might be. I don't know what else I can usefully do.

I still have no sense of time but later find out that Simon has spent over six hours in A&E, which is unusual. At around 10pm a woman called Jenny with kind eyes finds me to explain that Simon is now being transferred to Intensive Care and that she will be his nurse. She remembers me exclaiming "What, a nurse all to himself!" He is wheeled through a swing door at the back of A&E clothed in nothing but a twisted and blood-stained sheet, like a body out of *Ben Hur*. Esther and Trish help me gather up a growing assortment of plastic carrier bags and we head up through the corridors in pursuit.

I am overwhelmed by the quality of the set-up in what I will soon learn to call ICU. Simon is already in a side room with Jenny settling him for the night. There is a small waiting room for relatives which contains a noticeboard, a coffee table and some stained but comfortable chairs. Esther and Trish stay with me until Philip arrives. I give him a run-down of the evening so far and he sets off, ashen-faced, to get us each a hot drink from the café downstairs. While he is doing this a late night call comes in from Simon's cousin Heather. Would it be helpful to pick up his mother, who lives alone, and take her back to their home in Devon? At first mention this seems drastic, then next moment it feels absolutely right. I am adjusting fast. "Yes please, that would be wonderful."

I tell the nurses that I'm not going anywhere and will sleep in the waiting room. The staff nurse is clearly used to this kind of behaviour and organises an overnight bed for me in the residential block across the courtyard. Philip stays until around midnight and then, in a rather charming old-fashioned way, chaperones me to my room. We agree to meet for breakfast next day in the hospital café. I have a quick shower, trying with difficulty to wash myself with soap from the hand dispenser above the basin—the only practical detail that the hospital has failed me on, I note! Tiredness hits me suddenly like a brick, and the minute I lie down, I fall asleep.

CHAPTER 4

The city of St Thomas'

Like millions of people the world over, I pass by the outside of a hospital several times each week and rarely pause to consider what goes on behind its uninformative façade. In contrast, for anyone who visits, stays, or works in a hospital, it's an all-consuming environment that is as inward-looking as a cruise ship and as self-sufficient as a space station.

As a newcomer, St Thomas' reminds me of an ancient city, such as Rome or Marrakesh. There are the broad and brightly lit thoroughfares thronged with people of every age, race and culture, especially at peak times, and the discreet courtyards with seats and fountains, rarely chanced upon. There are corners where multi-coloured light slants in through stained glass at particular moments of the morning or evening, and myriad side alleys characterised by closed doors and private conversations.

Like any city, St Thomas' is a hotbed of commerce. On the main plaza by the front door you can buy anything from a newspaper to a soft toy, a 'Keep Calm' biscuit tin or a pair of floral pyjamas (one of the best selections in London, I note for future use). The crowds pore over rows of salads at M&S Simply Food as if in a Middle-Eastern vegetable market, comparing freshness and prices and sharing interesting finds with their companions. Only the haggling is absent.

The city of St Thomas' offers watering holes for every taste and price range. The main gathering place for visitors is the AMT café, open all hours, with a few deep armchairs pounced upon by regulars whenever they are free. I have always resisted the coffee shop habit, but now I can see its attractions. I quickly come to rely on this wonderful facility for people in distress: whether for emergency family conferences or for the solitary solace of a hot milky drink, for briefing friends before a visit or for swapping notes afterwards.

My other favourite is Shepherd Hall, a more traditional hospital canteen so well hidden in the heart of the building that it takes me a week to find it. Comfort food such as omelettes, chicken legs, chips and steamed puddings are served up at bargain prices. Its panoramic view of the Houses of Parliament on the opposite side of the river is one of the most spectacular in the capital and clearly enjoyed not only by medical staff and visiting families but also by savvy members of the general public. On several occasions I see the kilted Scottish piper who plays on Westminster Bridge walking down the corridor to take his lunch there, pulling his bagpipes along behind him in a suitcase on wheels.

This teeming metropolis of healthcare is the environment I tumble into just after 6am on that Tuesday morning: Day Two. I wake to a text from a meditator friend who keeps early hours. *"May your and Simon's minds be free from all impediments and completely united in bliss and emptiness at this difficult time and forever. May you dance and fly together in union in the sky of the mind. By your challenges may all sentient beings be free. Always here for you."* Andy's transcendent message provides a welcome moment of relief from the stark realities of the day ahead.

Twenty-four years earlier, one of the aspects of Tibetan Buddhism that had most appealed to me was its axiom that any challenge or difficulty can be transformed into an opportunity to learn and grow. I was also fascinated by the suggestion that the world does not necessarily exist in the solid and unchangeable way that we habitually take for granted, and that there are always other perspectives and possibilities to be explored. Here, when I am at my edge, comes a reminder.

Ever since I encountered Buddhism I've aimed to spend a quiet hour each morning exploring metaphysical concepts such as these. My morning meditation practice is based on the principle 'change your mind, change your world'. It starts with the simple practice of watching the breath, to calm my thoughts and—in the words of Lama Yeshe, one of my teachers—"to put the mind where the body is." However most of the time is spent reflecting on and re-engineering my mental habits. It was a revelation to me when my Tibetan Buddhist teachers introduced the notion that we don't have to be a victim of every thought and emotion that passes through our mind. My friend and teacher Robina Courtin describes it as getting back in the driving seat of a runaway car.

Just as my friends and acquaintances might spend an hour in the gym or take a jog around the park, this is my own form of daily workout. It is the breathing space where I get to reconnect with the ground of my being, review the day past, and firm up my aspirations for the day ahead. So as soon as I wake that morning I decide to head straight over to the ward and see if I can do my morning meditation alongside him as normal.

It feels appropriate that the ICU is as secluded and impenetrable as the inner sanctum of a maze. Tracing my way through some of the less-frequented corridors of the hospital I eventually reach the locked double doors and peer through their porthole windows for a sign of life. For the first time of hundreds I wash my hands with antiseptic gel, ring the buzzer and wait for admittance.

Once inside, I hurry down the entry corridor and onto the main ward. I hadn't been in the mood to look around the night before and am immediately struck by how otherworldly it is. Rows of metal-framed beds stretch the length of the ward under white-blue fluorescent lights. On each bed lies a body, a person, unmoving, flat on their back, and covered by a starched white cotton sheet. None of the comforts usually associated with bedtime are present. Instead, each bed is overshadowed by an edifice of monitors and machinery that whines, hisses, gurgles, clunks and beeps as it plays substitute for the vital functions of the patient below.

I slip into Simon's room and say hello to a tired-looking Nurse

Jenny. Ignoring a quizzical look from a passing consultant I arrange myself cross-legged on the floor by the bed. My colleague Esther has kindly supplied a poncho that will serve perfectly as a makeshift meditation mat. The last few hours of the night shift are generally the most peaceful time on the ward, and it is a matter of easy habit to slip into a quiet inner space alongside my husband. Simon and I are particularly fond of a verse by the Sufi poet Rumi: *"out beyond right and wrong there's a field … I'll meet you there"*. This morning Rumi's poetry comes alive for me in the form of an unexpected conviction that Simon and I are genuinely together despite the stark surroundings and whatever it is that is going on in his body. It is extraordinarily reassuring.

At 8am the shifts change and the hospital-city wakes up to its morning business and ablutions. Jenny is relieved by another nurse who tactfully indicates that it's time for me to leave. I make my way down to the café where Philip and I secure the two deepest armchairs for the first of many breakfast catch-ups. Philip, like Simon and myself, has worked nearly all his life in the voluntary sector. From his low-key appearance you might not guess that he's a widely admired expert on refugees and asylum issues, now in semi-retirement but still chairing consultations, writing papers, and advising at high levels. It is an incredible stroke of fortune that he has the time and flexibility to be there for us both. "In the best possible sense," he says, "I wouldn't miss this for the world."

The jungle drums have been busy overnight, and all day long my mobile phone rings and the text messages pour in. "I've just left you a message. I meant what I said: if there is anything ANYTHING AT ALL we can do just tell us no matter how small or silly it may seem. All our love and prayers are with you." Four London-based friends come by in the morning, and after lunch my sister Suzy unexpectedly comes into view down the corridor, having dropped everything to travel up from Brighton. I tell the story all over again, and she leaves me with a plastic tub of flapjacks. "I'm not sure I want to eat anything today," I respond uncharacteristically, but as soon as she leaves I find myself peeling off the lid and eating half the tub.

One of my biggest practical concerns is that my mobile phone will run out of power, so Esther kindly cycles over with my charger. Another friend has done a great job of informing the city clergy and sends a heart-warming email about how Archbishop Rowan has been informed and Bishop Richard is praying for Simon. The Bishop of London, Richard Chartres, has worked closely with Simon over the past few years and it's a boost to hear his stentorian tones on my mobile later that evening. "Let me know when he's ready for the consolation of religion … none of your Buddhist pretender stuff!" I've spent enough time around the Bishop to be familiar with his profound respect for other spiritual traditions so I know that he's just trying to bring a smile to my face. News also pours in of prayers being chanted in multiple time zones by my Buddhist community. It feels as if we are being held in a web of light and love.

Simon's brother Tim and his wife Mary Anne have spent the day driving down from Scotland. I meet them around 8pm in the reception area downstairs. It is strange to see them standing there, like a collage from a family scrapbook pasted into a hospital brochure. After hugs, tears and a visit to the ward where Simon continues to lie inert, we head homewards in their car. It feels weird to be exiting the hospital building for the first time in over 24 hours, leaving my beloved behind, and it's even stranger to get into bed on my own, but I am so tired that I fall instantly asleep.

CHAPTER 5

Medical unknowns

In the midst of all this collateral activity, like a mysterious absence at the heart of a storm, Simon continues to lie dormant. The illness that has struck him like lightening is located in the brain, and is so severe that it can no longer be trusted to run his body. Whereas in past centuries he might have been thrown into a dark corner of Bedlam as a strait-jacketed lunatic, or left to die thrashing in a cell, thanks to modern medicine he is instead lying sedated and inert in a hospital bed with most of his bodily functions reassigned to mechanical and electronic devices. His breathing is driven by a ventilator, he is fed and watered by a tube down his nose, his urine is collected via a catheter, and a plastic guard on one of his fingers (which looks disconcertingly like a fake nail from a Christmas cracker) monitors his heartbeat and blood pressure. He is also on antibiotics, just in case, and probably a host of other drugs that I never hear about.

I once read that doctors are like detectives, whereas it's the nurses who do the actual healing. Western medicine seems to have been particularly successful in researching and mastering mechanical issues—the heart and lungs, the flow of blood, how to stitch and mend bone and muscle—whereas Eastern medicine has focused more on the complex balance of elements and liquids in the body. It's a shame that with a few exceptions the two traditions don't combine their efforts. But even if they did there is a huge amount still to be discovered about the mysteries of the human body, so healing and healthcare is actually much more of a guessing game than most of us realise.

My brother David has now arrived to join the family team at St Thomas'. This is a significant bonus because he's a doctor himself and was even briefly a microbiology consultant at the same hospital. Brain illnesses and injuries are particularly hard to diagnose because the visible evidence is limited, diagnostic tools are still in their infancy, and the patients themselves can't provide any information about what's going on. David explains that the medical team are engaged in a process of eliminating the possible causes. It's a relief to know that we are in a top-class hospital, because otherwise you might easily wonder whether this is the best that the medical profession can offer.

The good news is that the third and most detailed brain scan, the MRI, shows no sign of damage. This means that Simon probably hasn't had a stroke. I find out that the reason we'd been so desperately trying to give him aspirin that first evening, by any orifice we could, was due to this possibility. As I punch the air and do a little dance I am gently reminded by a concerned friend that this kind of medicine is an art rather than a science, and best not to rely on any findings as yet. But no brain damage is surely something to celebrate!

Another possibility is that Simon has developed some form of epilepsy. When I arrive on the ward in the early morning of the third day I am greeted by the news that he's had a seizure during the night. Due to my limited medical knowledge this doesn't bother me too much, and when he has a second seizure later that morning the 30–40 seconds of twitching seem like a non-event after the much more dramatic events of the first evening. However the sombre faces of the medical team suggest that the implications are far more serious than I can understand.

For the non-medical person a lumbar puncture might sound like quite a dangerous procedure, but in ICU they take place on a regular basis as part of the on-going investigations. An attempt is also made to measure Simon's brain activity through the laborious process of pasting a hundred or so electrodes all over his head. This is carried out by two specialist nurses using a portable unit that looks like a combination of high tech and hairdressing equipment, with wires coming out at all angles. The problem is that in order to measure brain activity the sedative dose has to be reduced, which results in Simon constantly tossing from side to side and knocking all the electrodes off his head again. As his nearest and dearest I yearn to demonstrate a special ability to keep him calm, but am no more successful than anyone else.

After a few busy days of tests it becomes apparent that the medical detectives have analysed all the clues, followed up every possible lead, and are basically stuck. "Encephalitis", an inflammation of the brain, is the closest description they can come up with, with an infection as the most likely cause. It is a completely new word for me.

Since Simon's tests demonstrate that the encephalitis isn't bacterial, then it is most likely to be viral. As we know from catching flu there are many different viruses and very few treatments. My brother comments that he's relieved to hear that herpes encephalitis has been eliminated, because although it's one of the few identifiable and treatable viruses it is very destructive to brain tissue—basically, "it rots the brain." Some kind of reassurance! I immediately look over at my inert husband in alarm. The reality remains that with suspected viral encephalitis as the 'last man standing' diagnosis, nobody has any real idea of what is going on in Simon's head, whether he will recover, and if so, how long that will take.

CHAPTER 6

Family matters

"Your clerical friends have arrived!" announces the staff nurse, struggling to hide her disapproval. Two Anglican priests, the headmaster of a cathedral school (Simon's brother) and a lay reader (his sister-in-law) have arrived to carry out the ancient Christian sacrament of anointing someone who is very ill—and very possibly dying—with blessed oil. As a general rule no more than two visitors are allowed at the bedside at any given time but we have been given special permission for this.

Although anointing is a Christian rather than a Buddhist sacrament, I am happy to follow local custom. Over the years I have shifted from being a twenty-first century sceptic to someone with a deep respect for prayer and ritual, especially when it is rooted in a lineage that stretches back for generations. I also subscribe to the view that different religions are simply different paths up the same mountain. It feels like an insult to intelligence and common sense that the universe could ever be otherwise.

Not only Simon's father but both his grandfathers, his cousins and probably countless other relations who I've never heard about have been Anglican priests. Simon was the eldest son who bucked the family tradition. Ironically, after decades of working with homeless and mentally ill people, he now runs a charity located within an ancient City of London church and is regularly called to speak from the pulpit of other churches and cathedrals around the UK. When our wedding photos arrived, his chosen outfit of black Nehru suit and collarless white shirt caused quite a stir among some of our friends. "Wow, the priest is good-looking!"

We have many friends in the Anglican priesthood but when it

comes to ritual one particular cleric immediately comes to mind. Rev. Flora has curly red hair and is an incongruous mixture of High Church vicar and Territorial Army chaplain. Simon once asked her how she puts up with being patronised by the elderly men who she often encounters in her work for the Church of England. "I quietly remind myself that I know forty ways of breaking their necks," she replied.

Flora arrives at the ward dapper and prompt, a dog collar complemented by her customary Chanel-style suit and pearls. She is accompanied by her husband Jonathan, who is a senior army chaplain (the equivalent of a general, I've been told). I notice that his shoes, as always, are impossibly shiny. Flora's leather briefcase is full of religious accoutrements, including some special oil from Lambeth Palace just across the road, and my sister-in-law Mary Anne (who is a Christian lay reader) is asked to hold a small cross. I am pleasantly surprised by the profundity of the words, and by Flora's thoughtfulness in incorporating substantial periods of silence so that we can each pray in the way that works best for us. Flora later tells me that she felt honoured to be asked.

Simon's father was not only a priest but also a musician, so this is the other family ritual to attend to. Fortunately we have a particularly sympathetic nurse on duty who happens to have written her diploma thesis on the therapeutic effects of music on artificially ventilated patients. Tim produces a CD player from his car, and—aware of Simon's allergy to staples such as Mozart and Pachelbel—starts off with Vaughan Williams' *Sea Symphony*. I am surprised by the vehemence of my reaction. "That's far too vigorous!" I cry, in defence of the inanimate body on the bed. After a brief re-negotiation, we open with the soul-stirring lament of some vintage Portuguese fado, followed by the cheerfulness of a jazz version of *The Old Rugged Cross* performed by our favourite Australian musician James Morrison, followed by the serenity of Bach's *St John Passion*. All bases covered.

There doesn't seem to be anything more that we can do for Simon at this moment. This may explain why the family turns its attention to my welfare instead. They want evidence that I can switch off and look after myself, so I decide that I will give them exactly that. I book tickets for everyone at the midday screening of the final Harry Potter film in 3D at the BFI Imax, just down the road from the hospital. It proves to be a wonderful experience. For a moment during the screening I observe a flicker of guilt pass through my mind: to be having such fun while my beloved husband lies sedated and gravely ill in his hospital bed. However as distractions go, it works a treat.

On the short walk back from the cinema to the hospital we chance upon a festival of world food in the courtyard behind the Royal Festival Hall, and a pink double-decker bus wonderfully decorated with vintage bric-a-brac. Tim takes a photo of me lying on the back seat clasping a huge furry unicorn, which pretty much represents the strange worlds that I've found myself in this past week.

Each slow moving high-definition day and evening is a weird mix of voluble family life taking place on centre stage, with the demon of anxiety and despair lurking in the wings. Simon's brother Tim and my brother David have never had the opportunity to spend much time together, and one of the silver linings to this cloud is to see their friendship deepen as they walk and talk along the Thames. We're also endlessly sharing family stories and digging out photos of Simon that I've never seen before. One evening my sister-in-law hunts through our fridge and kitchen cupboards and cooks up a storm with all the food she finds. I vaguely hope that she didn't notice how long it is since I gave the place a decent clean. In the evening, bottles of wine appear on the table and my brother produces an excellent bottle of port. It's like Christmas, except that Simon may be on the verge of dying.

Back in ICU, my brother David asks if he can take some photos of Simon lying unconscious in his bed before he returns home to Bristol. The duty nurse agrees, although it turns out later that it's because he understood David to be a member of the hospital staff.

It's a rule that even family members aren't allowed to take photos of patients without their consent. When the staff nurse finds out that he's only a visitor she gets really upset, especially when she realises that David has also taken photos of the corridor and waiting area, and she demands that he erase the photos from his camera. David responds that this is a ridiculous example of political correctness, one worth sending to his favourite magazine, *Private Eye*. What he fails to mention is that he's taking the photos out of kindness in case they turn out to be my last memento of my husband.

After my brother's departure, the staff nurse shares her concerns all over again, so I ask Tim to make an apology on behalf of the family, in his best headmasterly voice. The next day, the consultant asks if she can have a word. "Of course!" we respond eagerly. "It's about those photos…" So much for all the effort that we've been making to gain the trust of the staff and to demonstrate how appreciative we are. Family!!!

By Sunday afternoon the initial flurry of family visits has exhausted itself. Tim is the last person remaining, and after five days in London he now has to return to work. I feel sad and lonely at seeing him go. At times I've been screaming inwardly for some personal space—it's a week into this ordeal and I still haven't opened a book. On the other hand, none of our family live nearby and I'm scared at the prospect of being on my own, especially should the situation go downhill.

WEEK TWO
STRANGE NEW WORLD

CHAPTER 7

Mortality

As we move into Week Two, I try to cheer myself up with the thought that Simon hasn't suffered a stroke or a brain tumour. He may be unconscious but he's still alive, and probably with better prospects than the thousands of people starving in the Horn of Africa. Death is all around us, not just in ICU. The newspaper headlines tell me that in Norway a killer has just gunned down 69 young people at a summer camp. In a Sunday magazine I read the story of a woman who has died in a freak wave on exactly the same beach in Mexico where Simon and I swam together the year before. Some of the time these reflections on the precariousness of the human condition help me to maintain a sense of perspective and to hold anxiety at bay. At other times they don't help at all.

On this particular morning, I can't get past the fact that things are not going well for Simon or me. Lying in bed, I identify three main anxieties:

a) I suddenly get a call saying that Simon has had a dramatic down-turn. In response, I remind myself that he could hardly be better monitored, and he's on every machine and drug that modern medicine can provide.

b) Simon gets a secondary infection. My brother the medical insider tells me that the chances are 50/50 that he'll get a lung infection in ICU, going up to 75% if he's on a ventilator for a second week.

c) Simon "may not be the same person when he wakes up." This is what the consultants keep warning me. Well, according to Buddhism, the whole universe is in a constant state of flux so he can't and won't be the same! But I'd rather not have any major changes. We all like and love him as he is (or was).

The object of my concern—or rather, the entire focus of my current existence—is now lying in Bed 12, on the right as you enter the main drag of ICU 1. As soon as the possibility of a bacterial infection had been excluded Simon lost the side room that we'd initially enjoyed and which had provided welcome privacy for my morning meditation practice and for events such as the anointing.

We are fortunate that Bed 12 is in a corner, which feels comforting, and that it has a west-facing window, although the events inside ICU tend to be so compelling that I've never seen anyone actually look out of a window. In any case, the drips and monitors around the bed obscure all but the occasional shaft of evening sunlight. On one side is a basin where visitors wash their hands on arrival and departure and a wall-mounted holder for the plastic aprons that we're required to wear, which tear off a roll like freezer bags. On the other side is what might technically be termed a bedside table, although it lacks any of the familiar personal items normally kept by the pillow.

There are four identical bed-stations in this section of the ward, each with its own attendant nurse. All the medical staff from nurses to junior doctors to consultants wear the same dark pink cotton top and trousers. These are entirely different from the starched aprons, caps and white coats that I had naively expected, and create a pleasantly egalitarian atmosphere. The ward is kept scrupulously clean by a couple of friendly cleaners. I am grateful for their conscientiousness – it may prove critical in keeping my husband alive. They even dust the top of the curtain rails every day.

Simon lies in a blue back-fastened gown under a white cotton sheet. His mouth is perpetually open to accommodate the plastic tubes of the ventilation machine that heaves and puffs above him. He has needles in both hands and arms, which are changed every three days and leave red swollen patches. The nurses have traced a line around each red patch using a black ink pen so that they can see whether the swellings increase in size. Some of the nurses seem particularly adept at making him comfortable, for example by lovingly placing his bruised and battered hands on folded pillows. For the last few days he's been trying to sleep on his side, just as he does at home, but it's difficult for him to roll over without pulling out any of the wires and tubes that tether him to the bed. I painstakingly ask all the staff to look out for the tell-tale crease between Simon's brows that indicates when he's uncomfortable or stressed. Even in his deep state of sedation, these basic physiological reactions still seem to function.

I now know that one of the drips is filling Simon's body with the anaesthetic Propofol, which is constantly monitored and adjusted to keep him at an appropriate level of sedation. When I arrive at his bedside at around 7am each morning, my daily greeting is "Hello Simon" (never treat the patient as inanimate) and then, turning to the nurse on duty, "How's he been during the night?" and "What sedation level is he on?" Every twelve hours or so, the nursing team carry out what's called a sedation stop, a kind of mini-experiment to see what state a patient is in without the Propofol. It seems amazing that the tap can be turned on and off so quickly, and in Simon's case I understand that the results aren't pretty. I've never been allowed to be present and I can tell they don't want to talk about it with me.

The consultant rota has changed and a fair-haired older man called Dr Jones is now in charge. Dressed in the same regulation cotton top and trousers as everyone else, and wearing white leather clogs, he immediately inspires confidence in me precisely because he is so relaxed and informal. When I ask if he'll be around all week it's oddly reassuring to hear him drawl "I'm afraid so", perhaps because of its normality. I find out later that he's the top ICU expert and has an international reputation.

One of the changes introduced by Dr Jones is that what I nick-name 'the bolt' has been inserted into Simon's neck. It looks like a plastic plumbing device and means that there can be three drips going simultaneously into his jugular. The advantage is that the patient doesn't need to have so many needles going into his hands, legs and feet, and that the bolt can stay in longer than the individual lines, or cannulas. However it also makes Simon more vulnerable to infection, suggests that he's being seen as a long-term case, and generally presents a much bleaker picture of our situation. My husband is beginning to look like Frankenstein.

CHAPTER 8

The kingdom of the sick

"We are all dual citizens of the kingdom of the well and the kingdom of the sick although we all prefer to use only the one passport," wrote Susan Sontag when she was being treated for breast cancer. Simon and I are now firmly in the kingdom of the sick.

My friend Anna has made the inspired suggestion that I should approach our family emergency as if it were a Buddhist retreat. This immediately resonates for me. With the exception of our two cats, both fully supportive in their own inimitable way, I have no children or other dependents and am therefore free to devote all my energy to Simon's recovery. I run a charity which I set up myself so I know from the start that the trustees will be supportive about me taking compassionate leave. We have spent most of the year organising an international conference in France, which is due to start in less than three weeks' time, but although it will be our biggest event to date I'm confident that my wonderful team can carry it off without me. So I decide to switch off and tune out from all engagements and distractions and settle into retreat routine for however long it takes.

Most traditional Tibetan Buddhist retreats follow a strictly-structured daily regime designed to ground the physical body so that the mind can go on its adventures: whether soaring into space (very occasionally) or (more frequently) clearing a path through a personal undergrowth of restless thoughts and emotions. My particular Buddhist teachers encourage their students to do retreats of three months and even three years, or at the minimum—for those of us with regular jobs—a month in every twelve. I've been quite slack about this since I got married, but have previously managed a full ten weeks in a stone hut up at 14,000 feet in the Himalayas and six weeks in a timber cabin buried deep in the national forests of Montana. Each in their own way was an extraordinary and life-changing experience in which the extreme solitude enabled me to dig deep into my psyche and taste the power of techniques developed over centuries to help us recognise and transform unskilful patterns of thinking and behaviour.

In this new permutation, I resolve that the external form of my hospital retreat will involve getting up at the same time each day (easy, since I seem to have developed an inner clock like never before), eating at regular times, and going to bed at the same time (again easy: midnight!) Another time-honoured technique for helping the mind to quieten itself is to set retreat boundaries, traditionally using marker stones or natural landmarks. I decide that my retreat boundary will be the small triangle of Central London stretching from the South Bank area around St Thomas' Hospital back to our home, a 15-minute cycle ride to the south-west. I soon find that the remainder of the city with its clamorous bars, restaurants, cinemas and theatres, its busy offices and shopping streets, fades away in my mind like a vintage newsreel.

Another standard retreat tool is to limit the number of people you speak and interact with, but I decide to let that go. As a first-time visitor to this strange new world of chronic illness I'm keen to meet and learn from as many people as possible. Like many long-distance travellers, I've always preferred not to research my destination in advance but instead to find out whatever I need to know as I go along, mostly through conversations with the locals. On this particular journey, I'm also acutely aware of my own fragility: I need to be drip-fed information at a rate that I can sensibly digest. I'm on such an emotional knife-edge that I can't handle too much at once. This may be why I develop a steely determination not to research Simon's symptoms online. Instead, one day I take home a gently-written hospital brochure about what to expect from a stay in ICU.

It makes depressing reading. Simon has undergone nearly every serious treatment outlined in its pages.

The ICU consultants are my top sources of information. They turn out to be much more accessible than senior medical staff might be on an ordinary ward, and unexpectedly willing to communicate. On several occasions we're granted what's called a 'family consultation' in one of the small private rooms just off the ward. I discover that for the best result my brother or another medically qualified friend needs to be present because they can ask more questions, seem to get more candid answers, and can translate any technical language that comes up. It also means that we can jointly examine and re-examine every crumb of meaning and inference in the café afterwards.

Junior doctors and nurses have clearly been trained not to talk much about the diagnosis but prove an excellent source of clues and circumstantial information. When pressed, they sometimes help me interpret the squiggly ever-changing coloured lines on the beeping monitor above the bed. Simon's nurses also have the responsibility to regularly type statistics into a computer alongside the bed, and now that I have established myself as a regular I'm sometimes allowed to take a peep at his progress—or lack thereof.

Unexpectedly, the hospital chaplain is proving to be one of my best sources of information. Simon was originally admitted as 'of no religion', presumably because it was an emergency. If there's ever another time, this will be something to look out for. However a friend and priest who works at one of the other London hospitals alerted the chaplaincy team at St Thomas' that they had a practising Christian in ICU. Reverend Mia now drops by Simon's bedside several times a week. With over ten years' experience in a job that combines pastoral care for both patient and family she's an expert at explaining medical situations to lay people.

Mia is the equivalent of the English-speaking café owner that an independent traveller might come across in a small out-of-the-way town. Her special skill lies in preparing me for what might unfold in the week ahead, which up until now has involved breaking extremely unwelcome news. I see our conversations as marking the place where the road either turns a corner or crests a hill. Mia helps me get to grips with the new landscape that lies ahead, initially with a sense of fear and desperation. After that I pull on my walking boots and trudge forward again, because it's the only option that I have.

CHAPTER 9

The human pyramid

Having no children of our own has both positive and negative aspects. I'm glad I don't have anyone else to worry about and that I'm in a position to give Simon my undivided attention. On the other hand, if we had children of a reasonable age then I'd no longer be alone: we'd be sharing every up and down, caring with equal intensity, and functioning as a team. And if everything went in the wrong direction then I wouldn't be facing the future alone.

Our family and friends are doing their level best to support me, in particular, three men who hardly knew each other beforehand. Philip, the best man from our wedding, has extended his role in the most remarkable way to be alongside me every morning without exception, usually in person but otherwise by phone and text. Philip has also taken on the role of keeping Simon's trustees and staff team informed about his progress. I can understand their concern and need for information, but I just don't have the bandwidth to handle this extra task. My capacity to judge and screen what I say is in free fall, and I worry that I could share something too honest or too personal that would later affect Simon's reputation and career.

Simon's brother Tim, who lives 130 miles away in Worcester, is the second person who I can turn to at any time of day or night. It's a huge relief to feel I can say anything I want to him, because after all he's known Simon longer than I have.

The third man is my older brother David, a wonderful brotherly presence for whom nothing is too much trouble, including cancelling almost all his weekend plans to travel from Bristol to London and be with me at Simon's bedside. He's a man of few words who is happiest when out in nature, so it's particularly touching to receive regular midweek cards from him in the post, invariably with an image of a peaceful landscape on the front and the simple words 'Thinking of You' written inside. There is one weekend that he doesn't visit, because of a commitment to attending the Rutland Bird Fair. It later turns out that on that one weekend away he met his future wife.

It's purely circumstantial that my three main pillars of support are all male, and sometimes I do feel short on hugs and cuddles, but I'm also wary of the siren call of female comfort and companionship: once I sink into that, I might never get my composure back.

Simon and I are both in our fifties, and it's painfully impossible for our two elderly mothers to provide the support I know they long to offer. Simon's mother turns 90 this week, and while we're usually very close I find it impossible to share what I'm going through with the woman who gave birth to him. I know she will be sleepless with worry. My own mother is in her eighties and travels up from Sussex bringing me a crumpled brown paper bag of runner beans from the garden and other small gifts within her motherly scope. She takes me out to lunch but changes the subject when she notices I am about to cry. She belongs to a generation that would never have cried in public. It must be exquisitely painful for her to relate to me both as her little girl, for whom she can't take the pain away, and as the adult daughter who may be in the process of losing her husband.

It's clear that it's only appropriate for a very small number of family and friends to see Simon in his present state, and then only if we can rely on them to be robust and discreet. Earlier this week I watched a man being led down the main corridor of ICU with tears pouring down his cheeks and his face contorted in a rictus of agony and despair. Word went around that a young mother of four was perilously ill and it seemed likely that this was her husband making his goodbye visit. I was unwittingly gatecrashing an intensely private moment, and it acted as a stark reminder that ICU is not for the faint of heart. I wonder if I will soon be in the same state.

We're fortunate to have a few family and friends with professional experience of ICU: not only my brother David and Philip's partner Mike, who are both doctors, but also my sister Elizabeth and cousin Beth, whose practical mix of savvy and plain speaking as former hospital staff nurses is more supportive than they realise. After decades of frontline experience, their view is that the human body is essentially mysterious, with extraordinary and unpredictable powers of recovery.

Our friends the Revs Tony and Denise both have extensive experience of working in hospitals and are unstinting with their inside knowledge and support. "Well-meaning advice? Ignore it! Just do it your own way!" says Tony. Sitting in the hospital lobby they encourage me to keep a journal for Simon to read when he comes round, so that he can piece together what happened while he was unconscious. In terms of reading material, Tony thinks that Simon would much prefer hearing what's in the papers than being read to from the Bible. As we talk, I absently fiddle with a piece of white card that's lying on the table, eventually screwing it up and adding it to the dregs of an empty coffee cup. It turns out to be Tony's missing dog collar, which is wiped down and put back on amid much laughter about interfaith harmony and collaboration.

On their first visit to the ward, Tony and Denise vigorously tell Simon all about their recent cycling holiday. I miss some of the story, but when I ask to be filled in they tell me to get it from Simon himself. On their second visit, they take me out into the hospital rose garden and give me a check-up. Exercise? Sleeping patterns? Appetite? Libido?! At the end, I ask for the verdict. Tony says my ability to listen is a good sign.

Our friend Sarah texts me to say that she has been having "a few tests" at nearby Guy's Hospital and would like to drop by. She has just found out that her breast cancer has returned after an eight-year remission. We sit on the landing outside the ward and indulge in an hour of raucous and riffing black humour, each trying to outdo the other with our gruesome medical stories and bad luck jokes.

There are a few friends who are clearly struggling and I mostly have to leave them to their own devices, knowing that I don't have any energy to spare. A refugee friend with a devastating history of trauma and loss explains over lunch in the hospital gardens that she finds herself consumed with anger that Simon, who has been one of her major sources of emotional support and encouragement in the UK, is on the verge of being taken away from her. We discuss how her anger at Simon's illness may be a displacement of her unresolved grief for all the people she's never been able to mourn.

I quickly discover the dangers of sharing every up and down with people who aren't in the daily information loop. They may generously absorb the worst of news—"He's been in a terrible state today"—and then be left hanging for days until another bulletin comes their way. However, as friends gradually return to London from their summer holidays there's something very cathartic for me in updating them. Richard and Kasia, who I've known for nearly 30 years, sit me down in a nearby bar. "Tell us everything. We want to know the whole story." It's a reminder that there are moments in life when it's the depth and solidarity of old friendships that really count, whatever the divergence in our lifestyles and interests over the years. I feel a tug at my heart as I watch them disappear home, back to ordinary life, while I head back to the hospital.

Our friend Andrew articulates my situation better than I can: "So every morning you don't know whether you're going to see him sitting up in bed or on the verge of dying!" His offer to visit me again, any time of night or day, feels so much more supportive than the people who are trying to fit me in around their other commitments. "Oh dear, we both live such busy lives" says one friend, and another—even worse—consults her diary while musing aloud: "Well … I can't come over tomorrow, I've got a hair appointment." I'm not in a position to get annoyed, as I could easily have unwittingly said something similar in the past, so I just store this away as a cautionary tale.

It soon becomes evident that the people who are the most helpful to have around are those who've done the most work on themselves. They're neither needy nor demanding, and are flexible to whatever the situation requires. I can cancel or change arrangements without upsetting their feelings, and they're completely reliable. In this unknown territory, where the main story is out of my control and I'm constantly at the limits of my ability to cope, the friend who phones or shows up exactly when they say they will is a lifeline.

·

CHAPTER 10

Blue curtains

When I'm on holiday I try to avoid sending postcards in which the sea is shown as bright royal blue. The sea is a nice enough colour as it is! However either through a sense of humour, a scientifically researched strategy, or supreme indifference this is exactly the colour that's been chosen for the curtains that hang around each cubicle at St Thomas'. In A&E the first night and now in ICU they represent the scariest sight in the world to me, at which all my philosophising and prayers melt away to nothing.

The purpose of the curtains is to provide privacy on the open wards. Sometimes they're pulled closed for entirely benign reasons — to provide a quiet zone for staff changeovers and clean-ups, or for visits from consultants. But at other times they're drawn to hide emergency procedures, or when someone is dying. Every time I come round the corner by the reception desk in ICU and see blue curtains drawn around Simon's bed my heart misses a beat.

For Miranda, the other much younger encephalitis patient on the ward, the blue curtains marked the start of her recovery. I was concerned to find them drawn around her bed one morning but the staff explained that they were in the process of replacing her ventilation tubes with a tracheostomy to allow her to breathe more easily. The next morning she regained consciousness. So when I'm told that Simon is also about to be given a tracheostomy, mid-afternoon on the Friday of Week Two, it seems a step forward and a cause for hope.

In any other circumstances making a hole in the neck and inserting a plastic nozzle into the windpipe would seem to be quite a major operation, but here in ICU, home of extreme medicine, it's just another routine task which is carried out at the bedside by one of the consultants. The 'trachi' is apparently much more comfortable than having ventilator tubes down your neck, and this in turn means that sedation levels can be lowered. In Miranda's case, she was out of ICU within a few days. Tracheostomies also reduce the risk of lung infection.

I am warned there's a small risk that the operation could go wrong, so as the dreaded blue curtains are drawn around the bed I head off to the hospital chapel. Calm and lofty, the chapel is located at the heart of the original Victorian hospital building and is the most peaceful place I've discovered here. It is accessed via a grand wooden staircase hung with the names of past masters, presidents, treasurers and matrons who in a strangely reassuring way date back to the 13th century.

At the back of the chapel there is a book of remembrance for people who have died in the hospital. One day I come in to find two dark red roses and a sprig from an oak tree on the page that has been turned for the day, held together with silver foil. On another day I find the chapel locked. While I am waiting for the security guards to bring the keys, a paediatric nurse comes by. She has just come off shift, and we have a brief conversation before she turns to leave. "You can pray on the bus home instead," I suggest. "I pray all the time!" she replies.

I initially wondered whether anyone would disapprove of me doing Buddhist meditation here, but my intentions are nothing but respectful and I've found a small carpeted area at the back where I can sit on a tapestry kneeler out of sight of other visitors. It's probably unintentional that the kneelers happen to be the perfect height for sitting cross-legged in meditation posture. On this occasion, any pious notion of praying for the safe completion of the operation fades away as I curl up on the carpet in my woollen shawl—just for a moment—and immediately fall fast asleep.

As soon as I wake, I head down the stairs and along the corridors back to ICU where Simon is lying in bed with the plastic tracheos-tomy tube safely in his neck. He is now able to close his mouth, after more than ten days of it being forced wide open to accommodate the breathing tubes from the ventilator, and is looking much more comfortable. On closer look, the trachi looks like the nozzle on an airbed. It's still attached to the ventilator but with much more scope for adjusting the volume of air and percentage of oxygen that's being pumped into his lungs and the potential for eventually phasing this out altogether. What a practical, flexible little gadget, loyally doing its work as the latest appendage to my husband's body.

Next morning I arrive full of anticipation only to find the blue curtains pulled tight. I wait for about an hour, and then unusually one of the nurses invites me to join the cluster of doctors around Simon's bed. I can tell from Dr Jones' body language that our turning point is not going well. Uncharacteristically, he's using his Christian name. "Simon, my name is Michael, can you hear me? Nod if you can hear me!" No response. Inviting me to join them around the bed is a last-ditch strategy: can Simon's wife bring him out of his coma? I long to be able to rescue the situation, to be his saving grace, but the answer is no. It's a bleak and despondent moment.

Dr Jones explains to me that the medical team will now adopt a more gradual approach. They will cease their daily attempts to bring Simon round on the basis that it's traumatic for him and fruitless for everyone else. Within Simon's skull the delicate grey matter which in its mysterious way controls our thoughts, memories and physical movements and hence pretty much our entire life, remains swamped in septic fluid and unable to function. I think of pickled onions in ageing vinegar, and give a shudder. All the doctors can suggest is to wait for a sign that the unknown infection has receded. The inference is that this is an unusually severe case of encephalitis with a much higher possibility than usual of permanent brain damage. Even the nurses seem to avoid my eyes.

It's evident that our best man Philip is equally downbeat about

Simon's prospects. A mutual acquaintance tells me that he has quoted a 10% chance of Simon making a full recovery. "Oh really?" I reply, paddling fast below the surface. Philip later denies that he ever said this. I suspect that he gets supplementary information from his partner Mike, the medical consultant, and I appreciate his discretion in filtering anything he shares with me. A few days later Philip is unusually insistent on having some time alone with Simon at the bedside. I take myself off to the café downstairs not knowing that he is bidding a private farewell to his witty, imaginative and creative friend, in the likelihood that after two weeks of lying there with a severely infected brain there isn't much chance that Simon's mind and personality will ever be the same again.

The only light-hearted moment comes when the doctors investigate why Simon's belly has swollen up dramatically and is now taut like a drum. I wonder what new medical horror story is about to unfold. They do an X-ray and find his belly is full of—gas! It is probably a reaction to the drug regime, and produces some much-needed Carry-On-style laughter at the bedside. Despite all their sophisticated drugs and machinery there's not much the medical team can do about gas.

For some strange reason, I feel relatively calm about recent developments. Of course I don't like the idea of not trying to bring Simon round each day but, unlike the medical staff, I know he's a person of great strength and determination who invariably pulls through at the last minute when least expected.

With immaculate timing, my musician sister Kate pitches up in ICU. Her own experience of recovering from meningitis and of playing music to palliative care patients gives her a special sensitivity to our situation. She's brought a small Tanzanian thumb harp with her and for the next couple of hours she gently plays and sings around the bed, creating an invisible tent of comfort and support around Simon and myself. We've been told that it's customary to seek permission from the ward sister for any live music but this is very discreet, and all the nurses within earshot are supportive, perhaps because of the events of the morning.

After Kate leaves I sit for a while longer by the bed holding Simon's hand lightly in my palm, and suddenly an extraordinary thing happens—he is gripping me back so hard that my fingers begin to go numb. I beckon for the nurse to take a look, partly because I can hardly believe it myself, and need to know that it's not just wishful thinking. After about 45 minutes his grip loosens but is still strong for another 45 minutes. I'm not convinced this comes from him personally: it feels more like a gift of reassurance and encouragement from the universe after our earlier disappointment. Even if Simon wasn't ready to come out of his coma today it's a sign of hope that everything will eventually turn out okay.

CHAPTER 11

A web of support

One of the many things I have learned in this second week is that one of the biggest challenges in any health crisis is how to keep friends and family up to date with the latest developments without becoming exhausted or distracted, and how to match their kind offers of help with what I actually need or can handle at the time.

Only the very closest family members and friends have been encouraged to visit Simon in ICU. It feels important for both him and I to keep the zone around his bed as peaceful as possible. However something particularly lovely happens on the ward one morning. As narrated by the ward sister, a man in cycling gear with a particularly big smile arrived with gifts of biscuits and fruit "for the nurses who are caring for Simon." I am touched by such quiet thoughtfulness and generosity, made without any kind of expectation or demand. I wasn't around at the time, and the sister apologised for not remembering the man's name.

Nobody wants to hear a telephone ringtone on an acute ward, so texts have become a lifeline. I feel very fortunate to discover a warm and loving text on my phone in almost every moment of need. As long as no reply is expected this is a wonderfully immediate and effective way to offer support. Although the hospital offers free wifi in the public areas I am reluctant to spend my limited energy on email. It seems I'm not the only one: the hospital cafés and other gathering places are full of real conversations taking place in real time.

At the weekend, I raid Simon's phone to get the numbers of some of his close male friends. We've always believed that having separate friends of our own gender is important to a healthy marriage, so these aren't people I'm close to but they nevertheless need to know what's going on. One of them is an old drinking mate and also an IT enthusiast and he offers to set up a Facebook page on our behalf.

His first posting gives me an outlet for the anger that I've been unknowingly storing up inside. Instead of making me smile, the flippancy makes me see red.

Okay Simon is in Intensive Care at St Thomas' Hospital. We will be trying to use Facebook to let people know what his progress is. So at the moment:
Visitors? No visitors just yet, he is in intensive care (watch this space).
What is he doing there? Hopefully, being looked after.
I mean . . . why is he there? *Alison to fill in*
Can we send him Grapes/Airfix Kits/Cards etc? *Alison to fill in*

Perhaps I'm getting my just desserts. Simon would wince at the decision to set up a Facebook group in his name. And he wouldn't be the only one. It turns out that many of our middle-aged friends find themselves overcoming long-held prejudices to open an account and join the group, while others choose to access it via their children's accounts.

I've always felt that due to our tendency to get absorbed in our jobs Simon and I have been rather cavalier about nurturing friendships, so it's a wonderful surprise to find out how many people care about us. There is a growing swell of concern from our friends around the world and for me Facebook turns out to be the perfect tool for engaging with them in my own time and at my own pace. Every evening I come home to a rich mix of poems, prayers, images and music, which I read and re-read with a mixture of smiles and tears.

Some of the posts conjure up the tangible presence of people whom I long to have alongside me in these difficult days. A message to Simon from his cousin Nigel brings that gentle spirit right into ICU alongside us, as if it were the scent of the bees that he keeps on his smallholding on the edge of Dartmoor. "*Take your rest. Allow yourself to be healed. Be carried by the huge wave of love and respect we all feel for you and Alison. Know that we wait patiently for your recovery and long for your humour, wisdom, inspiration and life.*" An old friend from Simon's beloved Hungary posts an MP3 clip of Bartok's *Allegro Barbaro*, explaining that listening to this piece of music is her own personal prayer for Simon. "*That very rough and intense will to live, the will to survive in some way, which is the core of the Hungarian spirit, may help You in these times. Much love, Zsuzsa.*"

I am also deeply touched by the tributes that pour in, even if they sometimes feel like funeral eulogies in advance of the event. Some tell me things I never knew: "*Simon was supportive, helpful and engaging (as well as very generous!), when I staged a fundraising event to raise money for an orphanage in Madagascar.*" Others elevate him so high that I hardly recognise him: "*If Simon may not be a saint, O God, he surely must be one of the thirty-six 'Lamed Vav' righteous human beings on the face of the earth, on whose account, according to our ancient Jewish legend, You preserve our world, despite its pervasive evil.*" Another dear friend is disarmingly honest: "*I went to spend some days with Simon last summer in Devon. He took me out on his tiny boat and he rowed all the way round to another bay from Kingsbridge. I would have been exhausted in about two minutes, he never stopped and the water was choppy as a wind came up suddenly. Ok, he didn't fancy rowing back, instead we parked the boat and had a lovely walk back home.*"

Simon's friend Alec from university days uses the Facebook group to remind us of happier times. "*This Sunday I am going to the Lakes for a few days with my son and wife for some spiritual uplift, and I promise you every fell we climb I will be saying a prayer for Simon. Years ago we walked the Yorkshire Dales together, Simon always encouraging our little group by telling us before each next stage "that there isn't far to go!" I shall be thinking of those funny moments when walking in the next few days. Simon has always had the capacity to make me laugh. Alison, however far we all have to walk to get Simon better, we are all up for it. Be sure of that.*"

To my surprise, one of the recurring themes in the group is

gratitude. Courtesy of Facebook, it becomes apparent that I'm not the only person who is undergoing some kind of personal transformation. One of the side effects of extreme situations is that they remind us of what is meaningful in life. *"It's paradoxical that this oh-so-serious situation has generated such unity and inspiration among such diverse people,"* posts a friend in Amsterdam. *"Thanks for offering us all this reason for connecting and focusing on what is important. We are many that are with you,"* adds a friend in Copenhagen. From another friend in Raleigh, North Carolina: *"Thank you for the opportunity to express our love to you and feel connected at this time. May Simon hear and feel your love and that flowing through us all to you both."*

A poet friend called Roger, who himself has extensive experiences of mental distress and hospital life, seems to sum everything up when he posts:

All those friends
all those prayers
medicine or spirit
wherever you are Simon
You will be safe.
And Alison

WEEK THREE
LIFE AND DEATH

CHAPTER 12

Self-care

"You have power over your mind, but not over outside events. Realize this, and you will find strength," wrote the Roman leader and philosopher Marcus Aurelius. For the past two weeks I've been living spontaneously, simply reacting as best as I can to whatever arises with the speed, intensity and fragile balance of a ballet dancer on pointe. In some circles this might be seen as an advanced spiritual state of living 'in the now'. Possibly—but it also makes me more vulnerable and unsteady. I am beginning to understand why hospitals put so much emphasis on routine, because it's something for staff, patients and families to hold on to in the face of so many big unknowns.

On the bold but instinctive premise that I am a key player in Simon's survival and recovery, I see that I need to pay better attention to my own health and well-being. What nutrition do I need, and when? What can I handle, how far can I stretch, and how do I restore my energies? What gives me strength, and what drains me or drags me under? When will I need company, and when will I need to be alone? It feels like there's not much margin for error.

In a bid to strengthen my resilience for whatever is to come, Philip suggests that I review my daily routines. We call on a friend called Lois, a management consultant whose speciality is to assist individuals and organisations in planning better. Lois and I come up with the following 8-point plan:

1.

Continue my practice of getting out of bed as soon as I wake (a steady 6am), and immediately making my way to the hospital while the streets are silent and empty. Enjoy a precious hour with Simon before the morning shift arrives and while the ward is at its most peaceful. Gather first-hand information about the previous night to help me prepare for the day ahead.

2.

When the shift handover starts at 8am, take myself off to the precious quiet space of the hospital chapel to do my daily meditation practice, in which I can dive beneath the choppy surface waves to the luminous and calm depths of my mind.

3.

After chapel, treat myself to a bowl of porridge with honey at the AMT café. On the days when Simon is doing badly, skip the café and go straight back to the ward with a bottle of strawberry milk—my staple comforter, which I carry with me constantly—from the M&S in the lobby.

4.

Spend the morning quietly at the bedside, often with Philip but discouraging any other visitors. This is when consultants pass through, procedures generally get done, and—on peaceful days—I can read some prayers.

5.

Midday: take a break! My diary is open to all comers.

6.

Back to the ward for whatever the afternoon brings.

7.

At 8pm, when the shifts change, greet the new nurse and briefly show them any music that I've selected for the night hours. Take the longer cycle route along the river, imagining the wind and water flowing over me and washing the cares of the day away.

8.

Return home. After supper and a glass of wine, go online to read Facebook messages and sometimes to check emails. This takes until midnight, when I fall instantly asleep.

To my surprise, I have no sense of missing out on anything. During the first few days that Simon was in hospital a speech bubble might pop up unhelpfully in my head—"We would have been on a train in Spain today!"—and suchlike. Now any sense of another life or different priorities has faded. It's like going on holiday and forgetting all your troubles, but in reverse.

There are also some advantages to this new way of life, which is unexpectedly giving me more space for reflection and for quality time with family and friends than I've had in years. For example, I'm thoroughly enjoying being a lady who lunches. Wealthier friends book a table at a nearby restaurant; other friends bring sandwiches for a picnic in the gardens. It doesn't matter which—it's all a break, a treat, a lifebuoy.

On the bleaker days when nobody's free or when someone cancels, I force myself to do something—anything—to unwind, whether it's reading a newspaper or staring at the river flowing past the hospital. In Week One I optimistically brought my jogging kit onto the ward, but now I feel far too fragile for that. I would fear spilling my tears and vital fluids across the towpath.

In the downstairs hall the hospital has organised a summer season of lunchtime concerts. Only a few of us seem to be regulars, but hundreds of others turn their heads to smile as they pass through. The quality of the music is outstanding. On one occasion a fire alarm goes off and beeps throughout.

In the evenings, our friend and lodger Sue usually prepares a simple supper for us both and—even more importantly—is ready and willing to listen to the events of the day. I later discover that Sue has evolved her own support network to help her with the gruelling experience of hearing my news every evening, whether good or bad.

A friend on the outside says with the best of intentions: "Good luck with the hospital visiting." Those inside the Kingdom of the Sick know that for the duration, the hospital is your home and the centre of your existence. It's the rest of your life that you're visiting.

CHAPTER 13

Pneumonia

Reverend Mia the hospital chaplain drops by for what has become our regular Monday catch-up and advice session. She explains that after Dr Jones' unsuccessful attempt to bring Simon round at the end of the previous week he will now be labelled a long-term patient. He may not be given the same priority by the ICU team and I will need to get used to watching other patients pass through and move on. These conversations are very painful but, akin to homeopathy, they function to give me strength by preparing my mind and body in some small measure for the difficulties ahead.

My original metaphor of travelling through a strange country isn't working at the moment because I can't relate to the idea of actually getting anywhere. Instead, it's as if I'm running around a racetrack where each lap brings fresh challenges and unknowns. This week's lap is the hardest by far. I don't feel I have the necessary strength to run another lap—but here I am, getting on with it, because I have no other option. My inner athlete is training with unprecedented intensity.

It's not as if Simon is showing any signs of recovery. On the contrary, his situation is getting worse. In the last few days, the skin of his neck around the new tracheostomy has become flushed and swollen and he's pale, clammy, and sweats constantly. I learn that the infection indicators used in ICU—white cell count, and something called C-reactive Protein, or CRP—are going up. It's soon evident that Simon has contracted pneumonia, which as my brother David warned was almost inevitable after so many days on artificial ventilation.

Because he is unconscious, the phlegm gathering in Simon's

lungs has to be sucked up manually through a tube inserted into the tracheostomy, a process that causes him to retch horribly. The more conscientious nurses apologise to the inert patient every time they do this. I watch as nearly half a litre of yellow phlegm is extracted via the hole in his neck in just a few hours, and hold his hand each time he retches just in case it helps. It is excruciatingly difficult to watch.

In terms of nutrition, Simon continues to be sustained by an unattractive tan-coloured liquid that enters through the tube in his nose and continues down into his stomach. At regular intervals the nurses pump his stomach to check that the food substitute is being absorbed. Possibly as a side effect of his fever, he now has a high level of unabsorbed feed (called aspirate) and I overhear a conversation about the possibility of putting him on something they call 'total parental nutrition'. This initially has a comforting ring to it but I soon find out that's not the case. It means that he will be fed directly into the jugular vein through the bolt in his neck. Neat and tidy maybe, but it increases the risk of infection and means that his gastric processes will close down. That doesn't sound good at all.

We struggle on. My beloved husband is bright pink in the face, the colour of bubble gum, and never stops twisting and turning from side to side. I mop his brow, collect more paper towels from the basin in the corner and immediately return to mop his brow again. I recall my parents doing this for me when I was ill as a child and hope that somewhere deep down he is experiencing that same sense of comfort. Simon's feet are deathly cold, so I hold them in both hands and gently rub them. It is a relentless and terrible day.

Simon is a man of great strength and determination, and I try to take comfort from recalling his taste for long-distance solitary journeys and all the other wild and crazy things he's done over the years. This time around the test of endurance is taking place in a dimly lit hospital ward, and I can't help wondering how much more he can take. For the first time, my instinct is whispering that maybe I will lose him.

In the evening there is a particularly horrid incident. The 8pm handover usually takes no more than half an hour and I decide to stay on, because it has been such a worrying day. At 9.15pm the blue curtains are still drawn so I ask what's going on. "They're preparing to move him," I'm told. "Where to?" "Only to the bed space opposite." Earlier in the day an elderly man had died in that bed space. I close my eyes and get a sense of it being haunted and off balance – a place of darkness, a place where Simon will die. In contrast, we have spent two weeks doing everything we can to turn Bed 12 into a place of light and healing.

Convinced that this could be Simon's final straw, I freak out. It's as if I'm playing Monopoly and spending all the credit I've accumulated up until now as a calm and undemanding visitor on the ward. "Simon mustn't be moved! For religious reasons, and because he's particularly ill at the moment, and because...." (shamelessly, every reason I can think of). After a few minutes of this, preparations for the move are paused and a ward sister comes over to speak with me. I haven't met her before but she asks me to trust her: he won't be moved. I cycle home, thinking: have courage!

The following morning, for the first time I wake at 4.30am, deeply anxious. For half an hour I try unsuccessfully to calm my churning feelings, and then I pick up the phone. Various night nurses have encouraged me to consider ringing the ward when I feel the need for an update. However it takes an age to get through to Simon's nurse, and when I do, I am only adding to her stress. She explains that it's been a difficult night. Simon is very agitated and hasn't stopped tossing from side to side. "Sorry, I have to go!" she exclaims suddenly, and puts the phone down in a rush.

Thoughts racing I lie in bed until 6am, which feels like an acceptable hour to ring our friends Tony and Denise. Between them they have experience of psychology, psychiatry and hospital chaplaincy, and both as friends and professionals they are magnificent. While not pulling any punches they gently and sensitively help me explore the situation from the perspective of both head and heart. We discuss how I handle the concept of Simon's mortality, as well as whether to go into the ward now (yes!) and whether to post on the Facebook page that we're in crisis (yes!).

I get to the ward at 7am to find Simon even redder in the face, racked by coughs and curling in and out of a foetal position. As I approach the bed he stops for a moment, opens one eye and looks at me with what feels like a deep timeless gaze, soul to soul. It is the first time he has done this since he fell ill, and perhaps it is his goodbye to me. Then the moment is gone, and the relentless tossing and turning resumes. I caress him, mop his brow and whisper words of comfort in his ear.

When the night shift ends, I make a special request that Simon be allocated a nurse who is already familiar with him for the coming day. I am overjoyed to find that it is our old friend Nurse Clare. With the support of daylight and the ward team she brings about a wonderful turnaround: Simon clean, lying quietly (albeit more heavily sedated) and back to a more normal colour. My dear sister Kate also drops by again. Together we sing, massage his feet, and intuitively recreate a sense of peace around the bed. Going way beyond words, we are doing whatever we can to help him pull through.

CHAPTER 14

Prayer surge

One of the most powerful and profound of Tibetan Buddhist practices is also the simplest. It is called *Tong-len,* which translates as 'giving and taking.' On the in-breath you imagine taking in another person's suffering in the form of black smoke. As the black smoke reaches your heart, you visualise it dissolving all your own self-centredness, suffering and confusion. On the out-breath, you imagine that you are breathing out love and compassion to the other person in the form of white smoke. Even if you start by doing *Tong-len* for a particular person or animal, the visualisation can be extended into a prayer for the wellbeing of every being in the world who is suffering or in pain.

Tong-len is my practice of last resort when I can do or think of nothing else. When my mind and emotions are at their most agitated it allows the intuitive body to take over regardless of whatever is going on around me. Everything gradually falls away except for the sensation of being the compassionate bellows of the world, connected with everyone and everything, gently recycling suffering into peace and happiness with every breath I take. It is the perfect practice for ICU.

The Dalai Lama, who is said to practice *Tong-len* every day, says: "Whether this meditation really helps others or not, it gives me peace of mind. Then I can be more effective, and the benefit is immense." Over 2500 years ago, the historical Buddha taught that deep down we all possess a natural peace and clarity of mind, but that just as a mirror can become covered with dirt, similarly our minds have become obscured by unskilful and destructive habits such as greed, anger and—above all—by ignorance of our true potential. All the different Buddhist practices are simply tools and techniques to help us reconnect with this natural peace and clarity of mind so that we can help others do the same and together bring more happiness into the world.

I became interested in Buddhism back in the 1980s specifically because of this affirming and empowering can-do approach. In my late twenties I'd abandoned my first career as an expert on nineteenth-century British paintings with the auction house Sotheby's to seek a way of making my life more purposeful and fulfilling. I'd had a taste of Christian meditation at St James's Piccadilly, and although it was too late to be a hippy I suddenly developed an urge to buy a single ticket to India and see where that might lead. Until now I'd been the obedient oldest daughter who went from school to Oxford University to a well-regarded job in the West End of London, so I was curious to discover what choices I'd make if there was no pressure on me of any kind.

I had no intention of cutting my ties with Christianity, my home base, but a chance encounter with some other travellers led me to a ten-day Buddhist meditation retreat in Dharamsala, the home of the exiled Dalai Lama. On my second day there I was invited to join a group interview with him, where I offered a packet of seeds from the garden at St James's Piccadilly and marvelled at his strong hands, earthy presence and warm laughter. I subsequently visited a series of retreat centres and monasteries in India and Nepal, where I relished how young people from all over the world were coming together, studying Buddhist and other philosophies, and discussing how to live a meaningful life. Gradually I realized that Buddhism wasn't just about revering the teachings of extraordinary religious figures such as Jesus and the Buddha, but about developing my own capacity to live by the same standards and ideals. At that point I was hooked.

The other compelling factor in my shift to Buddhism was the calibre of the teachers that I met. First and foremost there was the

Dalai Lama, who since I first encountered him in 1987 has become a Nobel Peace Prize laureate and an internationally respected champion of compassion and wisdom. I was also particularly drawn to the powerful and practical teachings of Lama Zopa Rinpoche, who had started life as the son of an illiterate and penniless single mother in the high Himalayas and now heads up a network of over 150 Buddhist centres in 30 different countries. These teachers gave me confidence that it is possible for a human being to function in a completely different way free from any trace of anger, ill-will, jealousy or miserliness, and to manifest an extraordinary capacity to be of benefit to the people and animals who they encounter. I never felt particularly drawn to becoming a 'Buddhist', but I definitely wanted to follow their example and become more like them.

After 19 months of study, practice and retreat in Asia I returned to the UK and for eight years worked with street homeless people. Working for non-profit organisations such as Crisis and Centrepoint was an immensely dynamic and enjoyable period in my life but on some level it still wasn't satisfying. I came to the conclusion that the main reason why the men and women I worked with were homeless was because we've created a system in which we fail to adequately protect and support each other when we are vulnerable. From that came the wish to help individuals develop more compassion and wisdom so that we can work together to create a better society.

When my Buddhist teacher Lama Zopa asked me to switch careers again and help develop a new Tibetan Buddhist centre in London, I saw this as a logical next step. From there I went on to set up an educational charity, designed to share the teachings on compassion and wisdom which I've found so helpful myself with a broader range of people from all cultures and traditions. In the course of all this, I unexpectedly fell in love with Simon, who comes from solid Christian stock.

As a result, inter-religious dialogue and prayer is part of our family DNA, and the bedrock of many of our friendships. From the outset, it was also an integral part of the 'Simon in hospital' Facebook group.

In the first week of Simon's illness, I was particularly touched by the following post from a Buddhist friend:

Please pass lots of love and a big hug from me to Alison and Simon in sure knowledge that compassionate Lord Jesus, the gentle mother Mary and the great Christian spiritual masters will be helping their devoted son Simon through this difficult time. Please let me know if there are any special Christian prayers to recite.

Our Christian friends had responded to this posting with a wonderful selection of prayers and poetry from the Bible, St Augustine and the Iona Community, which I recited at the bedside each night before leaving for home.

In view of the deepening crisis over Simon's health I now ask for a prayer surge, and the Facebook group becomes a treasure chest of inspiration from our Buddhist, Christian, Hindu, Jewish and Muslim friends. It informs me that candles are being lit at Lourdes, in Jerusalem, in front of the Dalai Lama in Toulouse, at the peace projects that Simon has been working with in Northern Ireland, along the medieval Spanish pilgrimage route the Camino di Santiago which we had walked together, on St Columba's Island off Lindisfarne, and in chapels, churches, synagogues, temples and cathedrals across four continents. I am told about an elderly woman who is stitching a tapestry and prays for Simon with every stitch, even though neither of us have ever met her.

Our friend Denise writes from the USA: "It looks like Simon has facilitated quite a lovely, extended interfaith prayer service! So busy, even while healing." Gill, in nearby South London, responds "It's a living testament to interfaith co-operation, and Simon as a visionary will be thrilled when he wakes up to see what he made happen."

Amid all the religious exchanges, one of the contributions that I find most moving comes in from an atheist friend in Sussex:

Dear Alison and Simon, my lack of faith does not allow me to post prayers but I wanted to say that I think of you both in the small things of daily life – and the rather lovely things, like being on top of the Downs – and am willing there to be a time when either you both come here and enjoy those things or we can come again to Kingsbridge and see some film on the projector over the fireplace whilst Simon types smart and witty and thoughtful notes on some other film made by an Uzbekistan director, shot in Fiji, about miners in Siberia. We loved that New Year with you both and would very much like to be able to give you such a generous, warm and easy welcome here. With lots of love from us both, Lucy and Nick.

I am also particularly touched by a friend in South Africa, who writes: *"// silence (but I am here also, and thinking of you both with love and compassion)"*

Our friend Rabbi Mark in Florida somehow manages to unite everyone, both believers and non-believers: *"As much as I believe that You, O God care passionately about Simon's well-being, the intensity of the caring and praying and hoping somehow magically and mysteriously and spiritually reinforces the shield around Simon and within Simon."*

We're basically trying everything. "I was very happy to hear that people were praying for me," the Dalai Lama commented when unwell a few years ago, "and even happier to know that I was in a top-class hospital."

CHAPTER 15

Desolation

It's Thursday morning in Week Three, and I am lying in bed trying to come to terms with my overpowering instinct that Simon is dying.

The previous day was long, traumatic and tearful. As Simon tossed endlessly from side to side like a fearful child I had begun to wonder whether my desire for him to live meant I was no longer a source of support but a liability. It's hard to be of any real service when I'm in constant terror of losing him.

My Buddhist teachers often remind their students that death is completely beyond our control, and that one of the most important things we can do in life is to prepare ourselves for the inevitable. The premise is that through familiarising ourselves with the imminence of death, and with each step of the death process, we will be able to navigate the transition to our next life in a more calm and skilful way.

As part of this training, Buddhist students are encouraged to contemplate on a daily basis the fact that everything around them will decay and die, including the people they feel most close to. So now I am being put to the test. I have no idea whether or not my Buddhist training makes it any easier to contemplate my husband's mortality because I have no yardstick to measure against.

"Simon is hanging onto the edge of God's kingdom, and whichever way it goes he will be fine," writes Simon's nephew Sam, an evangelical Christian. I find solace in any well-considered and time-honoured interpretation of the unknown, even if it doesn't fit with my own metaphysical leanings. The Buddhist proposition is that the lives of human and other living beings are a continuum rather than a brief one-off and that the most subtle part of our mind continues from life to life like the seed energy of a plant. However none of us

him a positive rebirth, and find immense comfort in rejoicing in the future life of someone who seems about to die.

In the midst of these inspiring thoughts and glorious technicolour images I feel a light tap on the head. I turn to see the Bishop of London, Richard Chartres. For the past seven years Simon has been the director of a project close to the Bishop's heart. St Ethelburga's Centre for Reconciliation and Peace was established in a medieval city church that had been largely destroyed by an IRA bomb in 1993. This is the church where Simon now works, with the Bishop as his Chair of Trustees. The Bishop's secretary had alerted me that her boss might drop by after a session at the House of Lords. Although it is less than ten minute's walk away over the River Thames I know he has a packed diary and didn't really expect to see him.

I update the Bishop about Simon's condition while his nurse bustles about her duties, entirely unfazed by the presence of a purple-shirted dignitary wearing an extra-large and very blingy crucifix. Bishop Richard has brought Simon the gift of a small icon of St George slaying a suitably writhing dragon. He says some prayers over Simon in both English and Latin. As we walk back down the corridor, I talk about the challenge of holding on to a view of ultimate reality—that whatever happens, Simon will be OK—at the same time as navigating the relative realities of hospital life and giving everything I can to the struggle to bring him back to health, millimetre by millimetre. "It's like keeping my heart open in hell," I say. Although he doesn't reply, I feel that the Bishop understands. He comments that the visit will help him visualize us during his daily prayers.

Afterwards, Simon seems unusually peaceful. With the late afternoon sun slanting through the window and plainsong playing gently in the background I take his hand in mine and fall asleep.

CHAPTER 16

Domestic affairs

The front garden of our house is really getting on my nerves. The bay tree in the middle has lost its shape, the hedges are tumbling out over the pavement, and the flowerbed is full of weeds. There's a voice in my head telling me that this really doesn't matter—I only pass through for a few seconds each morning and evening—but I also have some faith in the Chinese art of *feng shui* which advises that a messy front garden will bring further mess into your life. It seems common sense that our environment has an effect on the way we think and hence on how we choose to act. And I don't need any more mess right now.

As an experiment, I decide to come home from the hospital one Sunday lunchtime to do some gardening. It turns out to be a bad idea. The friend who offered to join me changes her plans. The initial pleasure at being active fades away as it begins to rain. The final straw is when an elderly man walks past, and comments in a friendly way, "You should get your husband to help with this!" I burst into tears so vigorously that my neighbour Jean comes out of her front door to see what's going on.

Jean invites me to join her and some friends for lunch. Her guests include a man whose wife has just died. He sits silently at the end of the table totally absorbed in his grief with no energy for anything except the basic necessity of getting some sustenance down his throat. As Jean pulls up a chair for me at the table I wonder if I will soon be in the same condition. Aware that I'm incapable of talking about anything except hospital life I too keep my mouth firmly shut. It's not too difficult: I'm finding it hard to relate to the chit-chat, banter and discursiveness that make up everyday conversation.

After three hours away it's a relief to head back to St Thomas'. The experiment has failed. Our house is laden with the traces and memories of weekend routines together and to come back to it alone has been a horrid experience. To compound this, I now have to make the mental and physical effort to cycle to the hospital for a second time in one day, not knowing how I'll find Simon. It is much more appealing to remain within the walls and embrace of the great hospital city and to draw on its many resources whenever I need to distract myself or take some rest.

Nevertheless, domestic life continues to make demands. The following morning a team of plumbers arrives to sort out the blocked loo in our upstairs bathroom. Two men arrive for the task: one young and technical, the other an older guy called Dave with tattooed arms who immediately inspires my trust and takes me under his wing. Another father figure—great! I'm collecting them as fast as I can. With the water turned off and the bedroom filled with equipment, I give Dave a set of keys and head off for St Thomas'. When they ring later to say that the loo is back up and running at what feels like an enormous price, all I can do is trust and pay up. The practical part of my mind tells me that I can't risk Simon coming out of hospital to a loo that doesn't work.

Another mundane task is to put in an insurance claim for our cancelled summer holiday. Friends have offered to help but I don't see how I can guide them through my inbox to hunt down all our various bookings, even if they might be in a better state of mind to calmly work their way through the maze of requirements. My first attempt to contact Ryanair gets cut off, so when I eventually get through all the automated phone choices and am told to ring a different extension I go into meltdown. "Please stop crying, Madam!" says the operator in a panic. "I can't stop crying, my husband is seriously ill in hospital!" It's very cathartic, albeit at her expense. When she breaks all the rules to ring me back—a phone call FROM Ryanair!—I manage to be suitably chastened and appreciative.

The challenge of recovering Simon's bicycle proves more enjoyable. On that first day in late July he had cycled away in the morning and struggled home on foot so it's a puzzle to be solved. Our target area is Waterloo Station, where he boarded his train, and members of the family have been scouring the streets with some amusing results. Simon's extremely respectable headmaster brother Tim successfully located a bike that met my description—a black racing bike with straight handlebars—in the racks outside the station. He opened the lock with Simon's keys, only to find that there was a second lock and to realise that the bike was a hand-made Claude Butler rather than an off-the-peg Ridgeback. Tim beat a swift retreat, looking over his shoulder in alarm at the bank of CCTV cameras.

Simon has always loved the Royal Festival Hall, so one lunchtime I take a prowl, wander past a rack where we've parked our bikes before, and there it is! I feel like a hunter who has tracked down their prey. The twist in the plot is that I've forgotten that he recently switched over to a combination lock. I try various sequences of meaningful numbers without success.

Our friend Paul is a very practical and helpful person who originally came to the UK as a Kurdish asylum seeker and who now works as a chauffeur. A few days later he meets me by the bike with a huge pair of bolt cutters. As it's broad daylight I tell a nearby security guard what we're doing and why, and then with one easy snip the bicycle is in the back of Paul's 4x4 and we drive it back to our house. Paul also looks at some other DIY jobs that need doing in the house before driving me back to the hospital.

DIY, along with IT support and cooking, is probably the most helpful thing that anyone can offer to someone in my situation, especially when they take the initiative rather than waiting for me to ask. Most of the time I'm too preoccupied to even know what to ask for. One evening I get back to find a plastic carrier bag on the doorstep. Inside is a loving note from my friend Della and a casserole containing enough hearty and comforting food to last for three days. On another evening my neighbour Jean appears uninvited but oh-so-welcome with a bottle of red wine and a homemade apple pie.

In the evening, I pay my first visit to a supermarket in over two weeks. Until now I've got by on what was already in the fridge, or whatever our lodger Sue has put on the table. I look at the multi-coloured shelves in a daze. I used to be a bit of a foodie, but now I couldn't care less about what I buy or eat.

"Check up!" Lama Yeshe always used to say. Can the mundane objects to be found in a supermarket or shopping mall really bring us lasting happiness and satisfaction? If not, then why do we devote so much time and energy to them? Instead of endlessly chasing after external objects and sensations, surely it makes more sense to redirect our energy into cultivating a more relaxed and spacious mind. A medieval Indian monk called Shantideva compared this to covering our feet with leather instead of foolishly trying to make the whole world smooth to walk on. Is Simon's illness putting me on the fast track to realising this important truth? I doubt it—but there is something in me that relishes the current rearrangement of my priorities to focus on what is most important in life.

Tim devises an elaborate scheme to bring his mother up by train to London Waterloo, then over to the hospital in a wheelchair, and then back to our house for the night. I find it heart-breaking to see this quiet and dignified woman sitting at the side of a hospital bed trying unsuccessfully to communicate with her delirious eldest son. "Simon, it's Mum. Mum's here!" I'm hopeful that he is hearing her on some level, but there's no outer sign to justify my wishful thinking. Seeing them off at the station the following day I have a fleeting impulse to jump on the train myself, and consciously have to hold my body back. Simon's mother asks me to look after her son.

CHAPTER 17

Non-recreational drugs

Rajeev has been our ICU consultant for the whole of this week and a rock of strength in difficult times. He is a tall slim Indian man who moves with the soft suppleness of a *tai chi* master and listens to everyone with the same old-world courtesy. He is clearly held in great affection and respect on the ward. When Simon's wires get tangled up one day, Rajeev immediately steps forward and sorts them out, which has the nurses seriously impressed.

According to something called the Glasgow Coma Scale which was developed in the 1970s to measure the eye, verbal and motor movements of severely ill patients, Simon is still in a coma. However it's not the peaceful state that this word suggests. Although he's unconscious all day long he thrashes from side to side, which means that someone needs to constantly be on hand in case he pulls out one of his lines or twists his catheter tube around his torso. Again and again he tries to sit up, and again and again I put an arm gently round his shoulders and guide him back down onto the pillow. He regularly stretches his legs out until his feet protrude through the bars around the bed and have to be gently manoeuvred back in before he twists an ankle. On one occasion he nearly gets them down onto the floor.

Rajeev is discussing with Angela the staff nurse whether to give up the struggle to stop Simon falling out of bed and take the radical step of putting him onto a mattress on the floor instead. This might also enable them to lower his sedation levels. They kindly enquire whether I have a preference. Nurse Clare had earlier shared a vivid image—straight out of José Saramago—of neurological patients being placed in cushioned indentations in the floor where they can writhe about without damaging themselves. Nurse Eva tells me that in Australia, where she comes from, Simon would be restrained. So a mattress on the floor feels like a good compromise, and I'm sorry when—for whatever reason—they decide to bow to protocol and keep him in his bed.

The straightening of sheets and plumping of pillows continues hour after hour, day after day, as well as throughout the night. I observe how our lovely Glaswegian Nurse Janet starts the day full of energy and optimism but by the end of her shift is clearly struggling to hide her stress and physical exhaustion. It is an impossible task for one person to handle alone so at least I can play a useful supporting role.

Up until now Simon has been dressed in the same back-fastened operating gown as all the other ICU patients. This constantly rides up around his waist as he twists and turns and has to be straightened again to keep him decent. This week one of the nurses has had the brainwave of putting him in a pair of the coral-coloured cotton pyjama bottoms that I later find out are standard issue on other wards. A problem that has caused endless bother is solved by one simple intelligent idea.

Simon is tall and fit, and with bare torso and loose coral-coloured trousers he looks like a warrior on a Greek vase, especially when he rises up on his knees in frustration at being tethered through the nose by the nasogastric tube. We still have no idea what is going on in his head but his great spirit shines through: dazed and confused yet unfailingly gentle and courteous. It breaks my heart to see my beloved in this state.

Rajeev takes the decision to wean Simon off his ventilator. This can be risky. We have been warned that after a long period of artificial ventilation many patients find it difficult to breathe unaided. However in Simon's case it seems to be no problem. Puffed up with vicarious pride I am the least surprised, because of my confidence in my husband's strength and resilience.

In addition to getting Simon to breathe normally again, the medical agenda of the week is to reduce Simon's drug regime. He is now receiving quite remarkable levels of sedation—more than six times what it would take to knock any of us out, Rajeev tells us—which could cast shadows over his long-term health. Apparently it's particularly important to slow the build-up of lipids in his liver. I keep quiet about the fact that I have no idea what lipids are, but the word is vividly onomatopoeic and it doesn't sound good.

One afternoon Rajeev introduces me to Debbie, the hospital pharmacist, explaining that she did her PhD on exactly the drugs that are being given to Simon. Debbie tells us that it takes at least 48 hours to test each new combination of drugs. I wonder briefly what Dr Masuru Emoto, the Japanese researcher into the relationship between water and consciousness, would make of it all. At least two thirds of the human body consists of liquid, and the medical team are dripping chemicals into Simon all day long without knowing how they will collectively impact on his unique physiology. Rajeev admits that he's been phoning around specialists in other hospitals, but that this is unknown territory.

On the Sunday morning, I arrive to find that in his overnight agitation Simon has knocked out his nasogastric tube and missed two doses of his drugs. Rajeev puts his head in his hands, visibly upset. "We spend six days fine-tuning it, and then this happens!" he exclaims. Replacing the tube is a major undertaking that requires extra sedation followed by an x-ray to check that the tube has safely reached the stomach. The upside is that the x-ray shows that Simon's lungs are clearing up after the pneumonia. However something evidently doesn't go right, because Simon spends the rest of the day wiping his battered and bloodstained nose on pillowcase after pillowcase, until each one is covered in yellow-red stains. It's wretched to observe him in such frustration and distress and be helpless to do anything about it.

This is the last day of Rajeev's one-week shift on the ward.

Sundays have a more gentle and personal atmosphere in ICU and we slip into conversation. I mention that *pujas* are being recited for Simon in South India and Rajeev responds that he was born in Kerala. I find out that Rajeev's father is a Brahmin priest and that he is familiar with some of the ashrams that Simon and I have visited. Rajeev feels he's too young for all of that. I respond that this is a characteristically humble Indian approach: in the West, we have no hesitation about striving for spiritual wisdom in our twenties.

Rajeev clearly cares deeply about Simon. At a family consultation at the beginning of the week this lovely caring consultant had made a bet with us that by the end of Saturday he would have him sitting upright in a chair. Even though the idea seemed preposterous at least it gave us all something to hope for. Instead, despite the best efforts of Rajeev and the ICU team Simon remains unconscious and completely out of reach, endlessly and deliriously tossing from side to side in his bed. Rajeev shares his view that we are now in the mysterious zone where the medical and the spiritual converge.

WEEK FOUR
VIGIL

CHAPTER 18

Odysseus and Penelope

I've now spent three weeks—or over 200 hours—watching my nearest and dearest navigate a private world that nobody else can access or interpret. To start with his only movement was the regular rise and fall of the chest as life-giving air was pumped in and out—a rhythmic process, powered by machines, which doesn't seem to qualify as breathing. More recently he has been thrashing about like an imaginary warrior who is fighting for his life. Meanwhile the rest of ICU carries on all around us. Shifts begin and end, shadows shorten and lengthen, and patients come and go, either to recover and transfer to other wards, or to lose the fight for life and pass into the next world.

Images from myth and fairy tales come to mind. Simon's spirit is absent, gone on a long and dangerous journey from which he may never return. I imagine him stranded on a distant shore, stuck at the bottom of a deep well or lost in a dark forest. Hospital wards, particularly ICU, are designed to keep killer germs at bay and in the process everything soft, comfortable and familiar is scrubbed and hot-rinsed away. Why would Simon be drawn back to this environment, I wonder? What can I do, as his beloved wife, his Penelope, to give him a stronger incentive to return?

We have already started with sound. Sound is the most basic and primeval of the sense objects, as St John (and many of the Tibetan classic texts) knew well: *"In the beginning was The Word."* Sound is also free and one of the few things that, within reason, the patient's family can bring into this stark environment. Bed 12 has a shelf alongside it and I have been allowed to commandeer the space on top of the shelf for "a few CDs." I bring new music each morning from our extensive home collection and take the equivalent number of CDs away each evening, making an effort to keep the music library down to about 30—a reasonable number, I tell myself.

In my role as Simon's personal DJ I select appropriate tracks for each phase of the day and leave a small pile of soothing albums by the bedside for overnight use. My most regular tracks are Gregorian chant, Palestrina and Bach, or else sitar, oud and qawalli music from India, Pakistan and the Middle East. My instinct is to avoid anything emotional such as Brahms and Beethoven, or the noisy Romany brass bands, Bartok, and Ligeti we've enjoyed together over the years. Various friends deliver favourite CDs to the hospital or offer to put together special compilations. The most common suggestions are to play Mozart and Pachelbel's *Canon*, both of which he particularly dislikes. That won't bring him back to us! Our singer-friend Carolina Herrera has made a recording of Spanish and Colombian ballads which I play so often that the CD wears out. She happens to be working as a doctor at St Thomas' this same summer, and one afternoon turns up in person just as her beautiful voice is weaving its magic around the bed.

Even on an open ward each bed seems to become an independent emotional pod where the patient's family can sit, talk, read, and— within reason—play the music of their choice. Only once does a seriously ill man in the bed alongside Simon use sign language to indicate, unmistakeably, that our plainsong is driving him round the bend. I have never turned a CD player off so quickly.

In between the music I read to Simon. Doris Lessing on cats, poetry by George Herbert, Lao Tzu and DH Lawrence (more cats), and Father Brown short stories. I get through an entire volume of Chesterton's gentle vignettes, probably more for my benefit than his. Somehow I'm never drawn to read the newspapers to him. On every level they seem too noisy and grubby.

One day I decide to focus entirely on Rumi. Our friend Amira in Sarajevo sends us a poem that particularly resonates for me:

Last night,
I saw the realm of joy and pleasure.
There I melted like salt;
no religion, no blasphemy,
no conviction or uncertainty remained.
In the middle of my heart,
a star appeared,
and the seven heavens were lost in its brilliance.

The nurse is looking a bit baffled, so I explain that Rumi is a Sufi poet from Eastern Turkey whose writing we particularly enjoy. "Does that mean you do a lot of travelling together?" she asked. Rumi would have liked that.

I am concerned about what Simon will see when he first opens his eyes, so I buy an acrylic picture frame that will neatly hide all the scary-looking medical instruments on his bedside table while being easy to keep clean. I fill it with images of Devon, of the cats, of myself with the cats, and with a postcard of the mysterious painting *Pilgrimage to the Cedars of Lebanon* which hangs in the Hungarian National Gallery in Budapest, and which we used as the theme for our wedding 15 years earlier. Painted by an artist called Tidavar Kosztka Csontvary, it shows a crowd of diverse and mysterious figures dancing joyfully under the spreading branches of a huge cedar tree. I have always seen it as a metaphor for our marriage, whether here in the hospital or in happier times.

The pièce de résistance is the whiteboard. I've always been drawn to whiteboards, and when I see one alongside one of the other beds in ICU my fingers start twitching in anticipation. I tackle one of the staff nurses. "Can we have one of those for Bed 12?" "They're in short supply," comes the reply, sensitively avoiding the question of why a patient in a coma could possibly need a whiteboard. "Can I bring in my own?" "No, that's not allowed." "Can I donate one to the ward?" "No, that would be too complicated." My eyes stray to the technical specifications on the back—how difficult would it be to source an identical whiteboard, and smuggle it in? Before I can expedite my devious plan, the staff nurse, clearly sensing a Wife On A Mission, miraculously produces a whiteboard to put at the end of Simon's bed.

The day nurse picks up the whiteboard pen, asking "What are the names of your cats?" "No, really, it's OK, I can take care of this for you," I respond, trying to be both tactful and firm. Of course I can take care of it—I've been thinking of little else for days. Within 24 hours, the whiteboard is covered with photos: Simon with the Dalai Lama and various other spiritual teachers, Simon collecting his honorary doctorate, and a favourite image of his bicycle silhouetted against the evening sky—a reminder of when he cycled solo across the great Hungarian plain. In the middle, I put a verse of poetry by Simon's late father:

I will go out and gaze on the infinite spaces
Of the unclouded sky
Beyond all colour and form and the changing graces
I seek His mystery.

Determined to avoid complete defeat, the nurse then adds a plastic clock, which promptly smashes to the floor.

On a ward where everything unique and comforting has necessarily been stripped away the whiteboard gives an unmistakeable message about who Simon and I are, and what we care about. On at least one occasion I find it being used as a teaching tool for student doctors on how to help their patients retain dignity and individuality. As the weeks go past, one of the registrars observes: "Simon is no longer simply the patient in Bed 12."

A few days later a new staff nurse introduces the idea of stimulating Simon's sense of smell. "Wear his favourite perfume," she advises me, "we've heard it can help." On the basis that neither of us are spending money on much else at the moment, I gleefully make daily use of my special-occasion scent, Penhaligon's Love Potion No.9. In reserve, I carry a travelling eau-de-toilette spray of my more modest second favourite, Sensuale from M&S, until the day that the spray mechanism jams. At lunchtime I abandon my retreat boundaries to cycle to the nearest store. There's a long queue at the desk, and I observe myself becoming hysterical. "My husband's in Intensive Care and my perfume spray has jammed!" A large and comforting M&S matron comes to the rescue. "I'm so sorry dear, please just take another one off the shelf." This also gives me an opportunity to purchase some more white underwear. I can't bear to wear anything black at the moment.

William is the new ICU consultant for the week and mentions that aromatherapy has also been medically proven to be helpful for long-term coma patients. I appeal to our Facebook group and am given the contact details of an experienced aromatherapist. To my surprise she declines to get personally involved, saying this is not a job for a professional, but for the person who is closest to Simon: me. Her advice is to purchase a mixture of lavender, frank-incense, rose, camomile and clary sage essential oils, which can then be diluted with sweet almond oil and used to caress and massage him. I purchase all the ingredients by mail order and set to work. Some of my early concoctions smell awful, while others are some-where between OK and gorgeous. At the end of the first day Simon shows no sign of appreciating my efforts but our nurse Katherine thanks me for providing such a relaxing work environment.

Simon's head feels off-limits, too fragile to touch, so I focus on massaging his feet and hands. Then one afternoon while still in his unconscious state he suddenly turns over on all fours and sticks his butt in the air. Acting on a hunch, I quickly rub my palms with oil and start to massage the area around his coccyx. The muscles are bunched in tight knots just as mine would be if I were stuck in bed all day. I rub in the oil using all the strength in my thumbs until with a satisfied sigh Simon turns over and lies down again. This occurs repeatedly from now on, although the nurses tell me that it's only when I'm there in person to respond.

Sometimes I worry about how the medical team are coping with having Simon's wife at the bedside for up to 12 hours a day. So it touches me deeply when Nurse Jane comments that "every bed should have an Alison."

CHAPTER 19

Battle of wills

One morning in the chapel a phrase arises unexpectedly in my mind: "Be still and know that I am God." I feel fortunate to be relatively comfortable with the term 'God,' unless it happens to be paired with what is, for me, the unconvincing image of a white-haired old man on a cloud. As Archbishop Rowan Williams said at a Christian-Buddhist talk I recently attended, it's important to remember that God is not an It. But what draws me is the essence of this advice: to relinquish attachment to any particular outcome, and to surrender rather than to stress and strive. I find it unexpectedly calming and serene.

As a child, I loved the Hornblower books. During one adventure, the entirely admirable Lady Hornblower proposes that there's no purpose in worrying about something you can change: just get on and change it! Equally, there's no purpose in worrying about something you can't change. Decades later I was intrigued to hear the Dalai Lama say exactly the same thing, and I keep trying to apply this same wisdom to my present situation. There's no point using up energy to worry about whether Simon will survive or not because it's pretty much out of my hands. Every now and again I feel I'm succeeding in not worrying, but then I lose the plot again.

I also warm to the Muslim phrase "Trust in God, and tether your camel." There's a lot of camel-tethering going on in ICU. Yet if God has chosen to re-order Simon's brain, who are we to argue with that? We had no hand in creating his brain in the first place!

Philosophy aside, my bottom line hasn't really shifted: I want Simon back, please, just as he was, so that we can continue our life together. And it's often the little things that get to me. For example, this week I am dogged by the incongruous anxiety that if he comes round we will no longer share the same sense of humour and be able to laugh together at comedians such as Bill Bailey. I see how much of our life has revolved around sharing small pleasures, and marvel at the fragility of that.

In my quiet zone at the back of the chapel, time, concepts and boundaries merge and dissolve. "Who is Simon, anyway? Am I trying to compress him into one static moment or memory of my choosing? That makes no sense, and will never work!" These intense weeks at St Thomas' are teaching me the importance of embracing the unknown. If I resist the unexpected, clinging only to familiar memories and concepts, then not only am I unable to appreciate what is unfolding but I also find myself brittle with fear about whatever could happen next. I recall the Japanese proverb: "*The bamboo that bends is stronger than the oak that resists.*"

Perhaps unwisely I attempt to share some of these philosophical ramblings with the Facebook group, and receive a storming response from our Rabbi friend in Florida. "*Dearest Alison. Although I am neither a Buddhist nor a Christian, my Jewish soul screams out against any thought that God in any way, shape or form decided that Simon's brain should be re-arranged, altered, whatever, or that God might have decided to afflict Simon. Any God Who would do such a thing I want nothing to do with.*" I can feel Rabbi Mark's explosive wrath from across the Atlantic, and decide it's prudent not to respond.

Meanwhile, oblivious to the theological debate raging in his absence Simon is going through his own battle of wills. Arriving on the ward just after 7.30am I can see immediately from Nurse Ed's shoulders that he is worn out—"shattered," he says. Simon hasn't stopped moving around all night long and looks equally shattered. There are dark rings under his eyes, and bruises on his arms and legs where he's hurled himself against the metal bars of the bed. It's clear that he desperately wants to sleep, but it's as if there's a chemical alarm clock in his body that wakes him up again every

60 seconds. I can tell that the nursing staff are unhappy with this state of affairs. They have the power to make minor changes to his sedation levels, but the general strategy is determined by the consultants, leaving the nurses to manage the consequences.

Simon's gestures and movements are becoming increasingly familiar to me, but he repeats them endlessly in slow motion. His eyes are now often wide open, but dazed and uncomprehending. There are moments when the expression on his face is so agonised and terrified that he reminds me of Goya's etching of Saturn consuming his children. At other times he looks more confused than scared.

All day long I whisper in his ear "You're safe, everyone's safe, there's nothing to be afraid of, if you're seeing frightening things it's only because of the medicines the doctors are giving you, you're getting better every day, we'll go home soon, I'm here and I love you so much." He lies back down, docile and peaceful, until the cycle resumes a minute or so later. I'm proud of the fact that there's no sign of any anger or aggression in him, just puzzlement and deep confusion.

One of the nurses has such an uncanny ability to get the bed comfortable and in order that I secretly label her 'the pillow queen'. She has the manner of an old-fashioned nursery nurse and this has a visible effect on Simon's behaviour. I muse to myself about whether this is an inborn skill or something that can be learned alongside the many other more technology-based tasks that an ICU nurse has to master.

Following on from Nurse Ed's challenging shift, the ward sister Angela assigns two overnight nurses to Simon's bedside rather than just one. I've never seen that happen before and wonder what impact it has on the budget. But to everyone's surprise, Nurse Lau and his colleague conjure up such a relaxed and nurturing atmosphere that they even find time to give Simon a massage, raiding my store of scented oils.

With the morning shift, the agitation resumes. Although still unconscious, at one point Simon actually gets his feet onto the floor. Angela is now at the end of her tether. She gets on the phone and negotiates to borrow a bed with cot sides from the paediatric unit. It's brand new with a brushed-cotton fitted sheet and padded sides, and is also longer than his previous bed. One side is missing its padding but this is quickly improvised using pillows held together by plastic forceps. Crash mats are placed on the floor each side of the bed in case Simon makes another bid for freedom and the bed is lowered to within a few inches of the floor. The entire arrangement is a triumph.

I don't know why I am so much less anxious than the nurses. Is it because I bear no direct responsibility for Simon's physical safety? Or is it because I'm unaware of all the risk factors for his long-term health, both from the original illness and from the drugs and other treatments that he's received over the past weeks? Or perhaps it's just because I'm closing down emotionally, out of self-preservation. The image that comes to mind is of a mussel that's only a chink open. However what I do observe, and Philip agrees, is that Simon's familiar gestures and poses are gradually re-emerging out of the fog. Despite the delirium, it feels as if he's gradually coming back to us.

CHAPTER 20

Travelling companions

"My pet hate," says a ward sister one evening, sharing a confidence while we watch Simon's bed being changed, "is the families who think that their situation is unique, and that they matter more than anyone else." I listen and take note, avoiding the obvious question: "Do you mean us?" I now have direct experience of how easy it is to be blinkered to everyone else's problems when you're holding onto your sanity and composure by the tips of your fingers. Whenever I do find the strength to look up for a moment, it's obvious that everyone who enters ICU is in crisis. Every family is riding a roller coaster, with their own back-story, soap opera of characters, and narrative of hope and heartbreak.

The hub of our fragile community of ICU family and friends is the Relatives' Room just inside the entrance to the ward—which through a Freudian slip I keep referring to as the 'Residents' Room'. The worn and grubby nature of this small space, which is hardly 8ft by 10ft, belies the emotional depth and breadth of what goes on here. It's a sitting room for relaxing over a reassuring cup of tea, except that there's no tea, no relaxation and little reassurance. It's an airport lounge for people who are waiting on experts and technologies beyond their control, but who have no wish to travel anywhere. It's a local bar or pub with its regular visitors and familiar topics of conversation, except that nobody is here by choice. The faded carpet is made of eggshells.

Along with the other long-stay visitors I watch the new families arrive, shell-shocked and teary, and can imagine that even a day or two in this place seems like hell. Within the week most of them are gone, before their application to our macabre private members' club has dried on the page. These temporary visitors can also fail to understand the discreet protocols of the club. One day, two young men sit together laughing out loud as they experiment with new ringtones for their flashy smartphones. They completely miss the fact that other people in the room may be trying to cope with negative test results, catastrophic downturns, and the lives of their loved ones slipping away from them.

The family of Miranda, the young woman admitted with encephalitis the week before Simon, are my natural friends and allies. Her parents have taken compassionate leave from jobs abroad and, like me, have turned hospital visiting into a full-time occupation. We are discreet about our past lives and intimate about the present—except when we intuit that our good news could destabilise the other's fragile ability to cope. I celebrate with them when Miranda comes out of her coma, while secretly mourning their imminent departure from the ward. My teacher Lama Zopa encourages his students to consciously and repeatedly rejoice at the good fortune of others as an antidote to envy and jealousy. On this occasion I find myself applying the antidote with all my might.

Other families have a different style. A young man appears in the bed next to Simon. He's covered in bruises, but when you look into his eyes there's a much deeper and darker pain. He is visited by two Sikh men who to my surprise stand rather than sit at the bedside with their arms crossed and sometimes even turn their back on the patient. On the landing outside the ward one of them opens up a conversation. "Is that a photo of your husband collecting a doctorate?" I assent. "You must be very proud of him. Whereas our brother, all he's doing is to drink himself to death. We can't even marry him off to a good woman in this condition."

In my first few weeks here the hospital corridors functioned as nothing more than a hurried route from A to B. Now it seems my capacity for empathy is beginning to return, and I'm developing a fascination with the carnival of people at different points in the hospital cycle. There are young women pregnant with the mystery of their first baby, hospital regulars with the strangest of bodies and the biggest of smiles, and patients and their families full of relief at finding out that their particular drama has a happy ending.

Wherever you wander there are stories. A woman in the café, probably in her late sixties, visits St Thomas' every month with her husband so that he can have his blood cleaned and replaced. They have learned to make an outing of it, she tells me. They go to the nearby Hole in the Wall pub for supper, where he's allowed just one pint, and stay overnight in a hospital guest room. The previous night the hospital had mistakenly allocated them a room with a single bed so they'd had to share it top to toe. "You just get on with it," she says. A young mother is enjoying a rare morning off from caring for her disabled child. She's chosen to spend it in the hospital café because she feels a special sense of belonging here, in this community of people who know at first hand what it is to lack ease and safety in their lives.

Walking into the hospital one morning, I encounter a young man in pyjamas who is smoking just outside the doors. Taking great care not to sound heavy or critical, I venture, "I hope you'll be able to give up smoking at some point: my husband's in intensive care and probably wouldn't have survived if he'd been a smoker." The young man replies, "Sure, but my arm is being amputated tomorrow." A few days later, there he is again, smoking with one arm, and he asks me for a tenner. How can I say no? I find that out soon enough the following week, when the ask goes up to fifty pounds.

Apart from the cafés, the social hub of St Thomas' is the panelled Central Hall, an open space located at the intersection of the main corridors in the centre of the old building. It's used on an occasional basis for fundraising sales of cakes, jam and second-hand books (organised by the Friends of St Thomas'), and on a daily basis for music. Every afternoon the corridors echo with magnificent piano music played live on a Bechstein grand situated just in front of the statue of Florence Nightingale. I wonder how they find such talented musicians to donate their time until I'm told that there's actually a waiting list, because few pianists can practise in a London flat without disturbing the neighbours.

"Friends, Romans, Countrymen, my kingdom for a piano!" says my favourite musician, a virtuoso Australian pianist-composer called John Boswell Maver. He is 79 years old, has flowing white hair, and dresses all in black like a jazz player. I ask him if he takes requests, and he pauses imperiously for a moment, with hands poised and eyes closed, and then launches into a Beethoven sonata for me. He tells how he once experienced heart palpitations while playing the piano here and was immediately whisked away to one of the hospital wards.

On one of my most anxious days, I wander down to the Central Hall for a free lunchtime concert. It is advertised as music from Serbia, Hungary and Argentina, with special mention of the tango composer Astor Piazzola. This is exactly the kind of music that Simon and I have most enjoyed together. I walk in just as the musicians are introducing the ethnographic work of Bartok—Simon's all-time favourite—and the dark-haired violinist begins to play one of our favourite dances. I stumble across the room, my eyes blinding with tears, and crumple in a heap at the bottom of the polished wooden staircase. Each successive melody brings more sobs and tears. I've hardly cried since that first evening in the ambulance bay and now I can't stop.

A family of three shyly approaches me, asking if I need either company or a handkerchief. They tell me that their beaming toddler has just emerged from four months in intensive care following the successful transplant of a kidney from his father. In this extraordinary place, which strips away all pretensions and disguises, I feel closer to my fellow human beings than I ever have before.

CHAPTER 21

¡Ultreia!

Karma Dagpa, the Tibetan sage who picked up on Simon's imminence to death the previous week, has made another, equally striking, observation. "The first month will be critical, but if Simon survives this then he'll be OK." Once again, I am surprised by my deep instinctive faith in his judgement. Having first established that, according to tradition, his reference is to a lunar rather than a calendar month, I batten down my emotional hatches and internally cross off each day that my husband continues to be alive. This is not something I can discuss with anyone else: it is my private conversation with fate.

Meanwhile the medical team has decided to check up on Simon's progress in their own way by carrying out a second MRI scan. The previous MRI took place on Simon's first full day in hospital and didn't show any brain damage. Nearly four weeks of coma later, the consensus seems to be that brain damage is somewhere between extremely likely and inevitable. The euphemisms flying around include "He may not be the same person when he wakes up" and "The illness may have left a legacy," but it's the bald words "partial recovery" that send the most shivers down my spine.

St Thomas' has a special MRI machine in the children's section of the hospital that is particularly suitable for patients who are sedated. This means that they have to transport Simon—in his bed—from one end of the hospital site to the other. The technical preparation for this outing is extraordinary: it looks like the run-up to a lunar expedition. An apparatus that resembles an IKEA bookcase is clamped to the end of Simon's bed with spare supplies hanging off it and a red insulated bag labelled with his home base: ICU 1.

Philip and I watch the gang of nurses and technicians bustling around checking and re-checking every detail.

In the midst of this frenzy of activity, I suddenly notice a change in Simon. He's lying quietly on his side with his eyes open, as if he's thinking. I immediately make my way around the bed to speak with him, and I'm sure that he hears me. Philip does the same. Everyone else is carrying on with their preparations for the MRI and is far too busy to notice. It's like a play within a play, with two completely different stories happening on stage at the same time.

Suddenly, out of the corner of my eye, Debbie the pharmacist comes into view. I rush up to her and asked her to come over to the bedside before it's too late. She asks Simon three questions, and gets a clear nod in reply to each one, clear enough for her to note it in his clinical records. Like us, Debbie is grinning from ear to ear. She holds out a hand to shake mine over the bed. I am suddenly crying, yet wanting to whoop and cheer at the same time. Debbie warns us that this is only a tiny step. "Wretched boy," I reply, "He's taken 25 days to do this!" Seconds later the anaesthetist's needle goes in, Simon is completely out for the count again, and trundled off for his scan. The timing couldn't have been more precise—and more exasperating.

Philip and I retire to Shepherd Hall canteen for tea and chocolate. Debbie had suggested a drink, but that feels premature. It's the first definite evidence of cognition that we've had, and we go over every detail again and again. We also agree not to share what's happened with anyone else.

In the meantime, there are the MRI results to cope with. My instinct is that they'll be OK, but when the significance is so huge it's difficult not to be hijacked by anxiety. Our current ICU consultant, William, has told me that it will take up to four days for the neurologists and radiologists to complete their analysis, so we are preparing ourselves for some nerve-wracking suspense. What he doesn't say is that the reason they need so much time is so that they can fully analyse the deterioration in his brain matter.

As it happens, I only have to wait a few hours—until the evening ward round, to be precise. William tells me that to everyone's surprise Simon's brain looks exactly the same as it did on 26th July. The results are so clear-cut that there's no need for any further analysis. This means that the recovery prognosis is good, although it will take an unknown length of time. "One day you'll walk in and see him sitting up," William says. In the meantime, he suggests that I continue with my alternative programme of care, particularly the aromatherapy.

Half an hour later I am cycling home along the river singing everything from "I could have danced all night" (*My Fair Lady*) to my old school hymn. No damage! Grey matter intact! My husband's brain is OK! When I get home, I break my usual rule and drink a second glass of wine.

At 11pm, the phone rings. It's the staff nurse from ICU. Because of the scan Simon had to be put back on the ventilator and the ventilation tubes have dislodged his tracheostomy tube. His nurse reacted brilliantly, immediately putting his hand over the hole, and Simon seemed to have no trouble breathing through his mouth. However William has decided that he needs to remain ventilated throughout the night which also means he needs to be heavily re-sedated.

I don't take this news well, especially after the extra glass of wine, and welcome the suggestion that the ICU registrar ring me back with more detailed information. Soon afterwards the phone goes again. It is helpful to get the full medical explanation, graciously given in response to my angry questions. "Why didn't they take him off sedation earlier?" (They wanted to wash him first). "Does he really need the tubes in again?" (This is what the consultant has decided). "Surely this makes him more vulnerable to infection?!" Bloody MRI, I think to myself. I stomp up to bed, angry and helpless. Mercifully, within a few minutes exhaustion takes over and I'm asleep.

The next morning, I'm tempted to stay away until the tracheostomy has been replaced but decide it's more important to see the ward team, apologise for my bad temper the night before, and re-establish my equilibrium at the bedside. The strategy fails. The consultants are busy elsewhere, so the tracheostomy doesn't go back in until lunchtime. Sedation levels are kept high, apparently because they're short of staff. Simon is back in his old uncomfortable bed, because the new one borrowed from the children's ward got damaged during the scan.

The Buddha proposed that however difficult the external circumstances, we have a choice whether to get angry or frustrated. If we do get enmeshed in negative emotions nobody will benefit, least of all ourselves. "Holding on to anger is like grasping a hot coal with the intent of throwing it at someone else: you are the one who gets burned," he said. I can see the logic, but the ups and downs of the past 24 hours have left me emotionally exhausted. It feels like someone has been driving a JCB digger backwards and forwards over my nerve endings. The best I can do is to settle down and offer some Medicine Buddha prayers by the bedside, both for Simon and for his new neighbour John, who looks in a bad way. Any remaining anger turns to sadness when halfway through the prayers John passes away.

It's such a rotten day on the ward that I almost forget about the positive MRI results from the day before. When I get home in the evening, I grumpily post them on Facebook. Almost immediately, euphoric messages begin to pour in from around the world. *Tears of joy today with your news. Tears from so many!*" writes one of my board members, who is helping to run our conference in France. "*Oh my god, I am utterly speechless. And awestruck. And how wonderful! (and mysterious – but that's Si all over)*" said a friend in Hertfordshire. From the USA: "*Thank God! Thank you, doctors and nurses and attendants! Thank you, Alison and all around Simon! Let's go, complete and total recovery! That's what we want!*"

One branch of our family had lost a wife and mother earlier this same year in ICU, and I feel particularly chastened by their elated response. Their test results would have been at the other end of the scale, and I can literally feel them breathe a collective sigh of relief for us. I reflect that it was worth getting the MRI done just for that. Yet here I am feeling like some kind of emotional Scrooge: we're not out the woods yet. From my current vantage point, I can see how readily we construct deceptively safe and reassuring worldviews for ourselves, like birds building nests in windswept trees. And, I add silently to myself, we're still in the first lunar month.

Inscribed on the inside of both Simon's and my wedding rings is the Spanish word *¡ultreia!* We first came across it on the pilgrimage that we did together across Northern Spain to the medieval city of Santiago, where we got engaged. We encountered *¡ultreia!* inscribed in wild splashes of bright yellow paint on the rocks at the tops of high passes but couldn't find it in any of our phrase books. Later we discovered that it's a medieval term that doesn't really translate into English, meaning something like "Keep on going, carry on!" Every now and again I twist my wedding ring around my finger and silently mouth *"¡ultreia!"* to myself.

On both weekend days, Simon is nursed by a tall American called Rick, who with cool professionalism successively eases him off the ventilator, the Propofol and most of his cannulas. The tracheostomy is now rigged up to nothing more than a small plastic cap, incongruously called a 'Swedish nose'. I can see this is a big achievement—back to where we were before—even though I have no energy to celebrate. On the Facebook page, our friend Roger picks up my mood exactly. *"From my own caring experience I know the uncertainty as things unfold. Know the hospital life."*

111

BREAKTHROUGH

CHAPTER 22

The second lunar month

The following morning the sky is a particularly clear and luminous blue. As I cycle to the hospital along Kennington Road, past the newsagents, the kebab shop and the Imperial War Museum, my mood shifts. It's the 29th day since Simon fell ill, and the start of the new lunar month. For the first time, throwing caution to the winds, I allow myself to believe that we might really make it through.

Simon has now been successfully weaned off Propofol, the anaesthetic that killed Michael Jackson, and it has been replaced by Quetiapine. A candid if somewhat tactless consultant had previously described this new sedative to me as "the chemical straitjacket that is reluctantly brought out of the cupboard for industrial cases." At least he felt he didn't have to sweet talk me. The new consultant for the week—a gentle and surprisingly youthful-looking man called Richard—reassures me that Simon's drug levels are high but not unprecedented: what's exceptional is the length of time that he's taking to come round. Richard notices the photo of Simon's bicycle on the whiteboard and confides that he is also a long-distance cyclist, which establishes an instant rapport between us.

Leaving Simon to twist and turn in his bed, I cycle away mid-morning to participate in a Board of Directors meeting. The previous week I had decided it was time to re-enter the world of work—both for the sake of the charity that I work for, and for my own sanity and self-respect. In between the hospital visits I'd managed to write a couple of Board papers and been surprised at how energising and enjoyable I'd found that. I had told the Board that I would be back at my desk two weeks from now. Various ICU staff have intimated that Simon will need to remain in hospital for at least four weeks after he eventually comes out of the coma, and this will give me the opportunity to fully re-engage with my work responsibilities. As Margaret Shepard said, sometimes your only available transportation is a leap of faith.

The Board meeting is in France so I am to participate using Skype. It proves a disaster. I'd checked previously that there was a wifi connection in the local Starbucks, but not being a coffee-drinker didn't realise I needed to purchase and register a Starbucks card to be able to access it. When I got a bit hysterical the manager kindly connected me using her own password. Not an experience to repeat, and a helpful reminder of my emotional fragility. This was followed by an electric storm of interference and long pauses in which I felt everyone else was talking among themselves or making facial gestures that I couldn't see. It was enormously comforting to return to the hospital and debrief with Philip in the café. I wonder if I am becoming institutionalised, and whether I will ever be able to pick up my life where it abruptly left off.

At my brother's insistence I visit my local GP surgery. I take the first appointment of the day—7am—so as not to disrupt my schedule in ICU. The appointment provides me with a sick note for my workplace, a sleeping tablet prescription (should I need it) and the information that I am eligible to ask for counselling for myself (should I desire it). What it doesn't do is provide any human warmth or empathy. My guess is that the young newly qualified female doctor is terrified of me taking up more than my allotted time slot. Her boundaries are as impenetrable as Alcatraz, and when we discuss the crisis that Simon and I are experiencing she could have been talking about a verruca.

To raise my spirits I come up with the outrageous idea of meeting my sister Suzy for lunch in Brighton. Over the past few weeks Suzy has been prevented from visiting the hospital by a cold, followed by conjunctivitis. So I decide to visit her instead, taking my first trip out of London since Simon first became ill. Philip is delighted at the idea and offers to spend the morning on the ward in my place. When Simon goes quiet at 10am after a sleepless night, I take this as my cue to cycle over to Victoria Station and catch a mid-morning train south. I anticipate that the journey will bring up some emotion in me but it turns out to be oddly matter-of-fact: nothing has changed, the world is just as we left it. My thoughts rise to the surface like bubbles in sparkling water as I look out at the people so busy in their houses and gardens, rushing around in cars, and disappearing in and out of shops. How crazy that we make life so complicated, when it's fundamental things such as our health that matter the most!

Brighton is huge fun. It's now a cloudless if gusty day, and Suzy and I have a girlie lunch at an outdoor restaurant overlooking the Palace Pier: salads, a shared veggie platter, and a glass of wine. We follow up with ice creams on the beach and a brief rummage in TK Maxx. It's my perfect frivolous day out. I buy a tin in the shape of an ice cream van filled with marshmallows as a gift for the nurses. I head back to the ward full to the brim with brightly coloured images and experiences, like a child returning from a school trip, and the ice cream van creates an entirely disproportionate amount of pleasure and excitement.

Suzy isn't the only person to help me raise my spirits. Our friends Sarah and John ask if they can meet up with me for the evening. "I'm sorry, it's not the moment for you to see Simon." "No, you dummy, it's you we want to see!" We walk over to the Royal Festival Hall, where somehow one bottle of wine turns into three, supplemented by the final dried-up sandwiches of the day from the buffet. My system drinks up the laughter and alcohol so thirstily that I don't even have a headache the next day.

Perhaps my capacity for anguish and suspense is temporarily exhausted. The body has its own intelligence about what's going on and what it needs to be able to pace itself. This whole business is so far outside my control that all I can do is hang on in for the ride.

CHAPTER 23

Patience

"One step forward, two steps back," cautions the staff nurse. "That's what we say in ICU." I am about to query her—surely, two steps forward, one back?—until I realise that she means what she says. Simon's infection indicators are up again (white blood cells at 30, CRP over 240) most likely due to a urinary tract infection. It's hardly surprising, they tell me, after nearly a month of lying in bed with a tube up his penis. When Simon is agitated we often have to pass the catheter bag, nicknamed the 'golden handbag', backwards and forwards across the bed to avoid it getting coiled around his torso. Apparently this also heightens the risk of infection. He doesn't have a fever this morning, or look as ill as he did with pneumonia, but I've been told many times that it's usually the infections that kill people in ICU. We need to get him out of here!

The nursing team are visibly concerned and frustrated by the lack of progress. I have joked with them about my husband's appalling record for punctuality and suggested this means he's bound to take his time. My instinct is to say, "Don't panic, things are moving slowly in the right direction, just be patient," but their mood is beginning to rub off on me. For the first time I sense an emotional mood in Simon as well: worn out, fed up, and just as frustrated as the rest of us.

I have to keep reminding myself that if it wasn't for the threat of infection that looms over every ICU bed then we can be cautiously optimistic about how the situation is unfolding. Simon is still extremely agitated (on one occasion, he doesn't stop moving for 48 hours) but at least this means there's no risk of bedsores and it's keeping his muscles in shape. Instead of an endlessly bleeping monitor above the bed, his vital signs (SATs, blood pressure, heart and breathing) are only measured every 4 hours. He doesn't really need the tracheostomy tube either, except as a precaution to stop him choking on his own bodily fluids.

In the short gaps between his incessant twisting and turning he seems more lucid. With eyes wide open he looks at the ceiling with an expression of either thoughtfulness or despair, and occasionally responds to the music that I play to him with a characteristic lift of his eyebrows. It's him all right, albeit shrouded by a thick and impenetrable fog. But there are still no "appropriate responses"— he can't open his eyes or mouth on request, or hold my hand. One afternoon he suddenly curls up against me for a few seconds, head on my shoulder and arm draped over mine. Who knows what is going on in his head?

One day Simon makes two large poos, which create an incredible mess and mean that the poor nurse on duty has to change all his bedding twice over. I am there for the first one and watch him make a desperate lunge to get out the bed. I'm sure he knows what's going on.

Simon is also achieving some remarkable physical feats, despite his unconscious state. The ward has its own team of physiotherapists who come round every few days to manipulate his arms and chest. One of them, called John, has taken a particular interest in Simon's case and today he says I can stay and help.

John sits next to the bed in an ordinary upright chair, legs braced apart, and at the command "Sit!" the nurse swings Simon's legs down onto the floor. Despite being unconscious and with eyes closed he is sitting up! I am fascinated by the look of concentration on my husband's face. John then changes his single-word command to "Stand!" and with a bit of a prod Simon tucks his butt in and wobbles onto his feet. Within a few minutes he's clearly wiped out by the effort, and collapses back into bed. We are all elated, and when the nurse shares the news with Richard the consultant during his evening round he thinks we're kidding him.

Encouraged by these indications of cognition, I spend much of the day whispering in Simon's ear, reminding him of all the lovely things to come back for. I talk about our cats and our shared love of Devon, and list all our family and friends one by one. I remind him of favourite London haunts such as the National Film Theatre, the Royal Festival Hall and Gabi's delicatessen in Charing Cross Road, and of how much he enjoys reading the London Review of Books. I also promise him that as soon as he comes home we are going to get the liver-and-onion-coloured springer spaniel that he has longed for all his life.

Sometimes I sense he enjoys me whispering in his ear and giving him massages, and at other times my instinct is that he'd prefer to be left alone, both of which are equally idiosyncratic responses. It's still a waiting game, but I am cautiously optimistic that Simon Keyes is slowly coming back to life.

CHAPTER 24

Saints and heroes

I now understand why people fall in love with nurses. I am constantly amazed by the never-ending stream of beautiful men and women who take care of Simon. In addition to English nurses from both town and countryside, there are the soft accents of Scotland, Wales and Northern Ireland, the beaming warmth of the Philippines, the laconic wit of North America, and even the occasional visitors from the Antipodes coming through in transit like migratory birds. ICU attracts the elite of the profession and almost without exception the nursing staff are not only highly skilled and knowledgeable but also immensely attractive to look at.

In quiet moments the nurses sometimes open up about themselves. Some are motivated by religious faith, although they're not allowed to talk about this unless asked. Others are at the beginning of an ambitious career. Rick the American nurse is delighted that he's just been accepted for a job in the trauma ward at the London Hospital, where he will be able to combine his experience in intensive care with the even more dramatic needs of accident victims.

When I cheerily say to a departing nurse "Have a nice evening!" I'm told that if you're on shift again the following day, you don't risk even a glass of wine with your supper. I am enraged to discover that the majority carry the burden of student loans from their years of studying for the nursing degrees that equip them to do this vital and life-saving work. Many are boarding with their parents in satellite towns because they can't afford to live near the central London hospitals they serve—even though these same hospitals can't function without them.

I had always assumed that nurses are constantly thanked and

presented with flowers and chocolates but that rarely seems to happen these days. I find out that there has been an alarming rise in the number of patients who verbally abuse the people who are caring for them. One evening a nurse overhears me talking in the corridor with another ICU family about what a wonderful service the staff are providing. She comes running after me to express how much this means to her, because "we don't get thanked very often."

As Nurse Jenny explained to my surprise on that first night, in ICU there is one nurse to one bed. My guess is that this is part of the appeal of the job. This is extreme nursing. There are no meals to serve, no TVs to adjust, no buzzers to answer. Instead, each nurse carries a minute by minute responsibility for the life of the person in their care, which more often than not is hanging by a thread.

One of our favourite nurses is a young man called Peter. One day he refers to me as an angel, so after that we always call him 'archangel'. Archangel Peter can't be more than 25 years old and yet he's in complete command of Bed 12 for the day, and of all the machinery and drugs that go with it – the medical equivalent of Captain Kirk on the Starship Enterprise.

Nurse Gloria is at the other end of the scale. Unusually for ICU, she's an agency nurse, a large elderly woman who moves slowly and clearly isn't at ease with all the technical gizmos that surround his bed. When she comes on duty during one of Simon's worse evenings it sets off all kinds of alarm bells for me. However when I return at 7am Simon is neat, tidy, and much more peaceful than the evening before. I approach Nurse Gloria, who is hunched over the computer alongside him, typing up her overnight report with two fingers. "How did you get him so calm?" I ask. "I don't like all these artificial contraptions," she replies, "so I just gave him a good wash with soap and water, and settled him down." She admitted that she'd also done some dancing during the night for the emaciated young man in the opposite bed "because he likes music, and it made him laugh."

It's tempting to get over-attached to the nurses, especially when I spend most of a 12-hour shift one-on-one with them. The manager in me can see that the staff nurses are alert to the risk of distraught families transferring their emotions onto their team, and of the staff themselves becoming emotionally over-involved. This may be one of the reasons why the ICU team revolves constantly around three different wards: two at St Thomas', and one at nearby Guy's. At first I am gutted when Jenny, Ed, Peter and Rick appear to desert us. However I quickly learn to relax and keep an open mind as other nurses with an equally dazzling blend of warmth, skill and kindness arrive to take their place.

Inevitably there are exceptions. Only once do I ask for Simon's nurse to be swapped for someone else. It is a particularly bad day for him, and my heart falls when a young male nurse arrives for the morning handover. I remember him well for chatting about cycling while leaning over Simon's unconscious body and for waking him up to clean his teeth just as he'd fallen into a badly needed sleep. Everyone has their slack moments, and in other wards these would hardly be cardinal sins, but in ICU I've come to expect a higher level of observation and sensitivity.

On another occasion, I am shocked to see two young agency nurses at our end of the ward chatting with each other and sharing a bag of crisps. Again, my standards have been set very high. ICU nurses work a heroic 12-hour shift, with half an hour for lunch and—if they're lucky—two short breaks for tea or coffee. They're not allowed to eat or drink anything at the bedside, so the takeaway drinks and snacks that sustain so many of us through a long and demanding working day are off the radar.

Some of the nurses are happy to give me minor support tasks, such as washing Simon's hair with a special shower cap that is filled with shampoo and heated up in a microwave, like the end-of-meal towel in an Indian restaurant. On other occasions I prove a useful source of information about their patient. One morning I arrive to find the nurse clearly in distress. "I'm so sorry, your husband's front tooth fell out when I was cleaning his mouth this morning." She was shocked to hear that this had also happened a few months previously on a street in Mexico, and that Simon had simply wiped the wobbly crown down and put it back in his mouth.

While the ICU consultants are warm and approachable, the other consultants who visit the ward from time to time rarely acknowledge or speak to me. Wearing white coats and accompanied by a respectful retinue of medical students they sometimes appear more interested in the illness than the patient. Dr Jones the senior ICU consultant is characteristically relaxed about this phenomenon. "They'll come up with all kinds of ideas," he told me, "but here we're simple folk, just trying to look after your husband until he gets better."

To an observer, the fact that the ICU consultants rotate around the wards on a weekly basis is both an advantage and a disadvantage. It means that I am constantly building new relationships, usually later in the week when a consultant has settled in and is less busy. I feel it gives me more of a role in providing continuity about the more intuitive aspects of Simon's care and ensuring that his background and personality are part of the picture. It also means that there's a fresh mind and perspective on Simon's case each week, and if I have less rapport with a particular consultant I know they will soon pass on.

I've been advised that it's best not to get involved in the details of Simon's care, but as our doctor friend Carolina warns me one day across the bed, "You're going to become an expert on things you never wanted to know about." I've found it impossible not to keep my own mental log of his sedation levels or to take my eye off the throbbing iridescent lines on the monitor above the bed, and I'm getting used to shorthand such as SATs and CRP. "You're either medical, or you've been here too long," a registrar says to me one day. "Too long!" was all I could reply. However there are also days when I need to remind myself to be humble: I may know Simon better than anyone else here, but I only understand a fraction of the treatment that he is receiving.

Coming back from lunch one day, I bump into one of the doctors from that first evening in A&E, whom I remember as being particularly kind. To my surprise he recognises me. "I'd never want to go through what you experienced that evening," he says. Why do I find that so comforting? I wonder to myself. Partly because it affirms the intensity of the experience. It's also because that doctor was willing to transcend personal and professional boundaries and to speak to me from the heart as a fellow human being. For him it may have been a small gesture, but for me it is one of the special moments that help me keep going in this stark landscape.

CHAPTER 25

The blanket

Each day I wake at 6am, put on a cotton sundress (because it's so warm in ICU) and my sparkly flip flops (comfy and cheering in the long corridors), pick up my backpack (stuffed with everything a girl could need for a day on the ward) and get on my bike. At every red traffic light, I wonder if my husband will still be alive when I arrive at the hospital, and if so, in what shape. Even though the wind now seems to be blowing in our favour I have enough experience of intensive care to know that the prognosis can change in an instant. Although I have permission to ring the ward from home, if I start doing that I fear the gaps between calls would drive me insane. Strangely, it seems easier to take the whole night off.

Except that this morning is different—completely different. As always, I climb the stairs to ICU 1, gel my hands and wait for the buzzer that opens the double doors. I continue past the Relatives Room, down the main corridor, and turn right to Bed 12. And there in the corner is my husband—sleeping! Peacefully, naturally, curled up just as he would be at home! "I asked if he was cold, and he nodded, so I put a blanket over him," explains a new nurse called Marian Most people in ICU are too ill for blankets, and they're made of a thin and comfortless cotton fabric chosen for its ability to survive a high temperature wash—but still, a blanket! Simon is also snoring gently, for the first time in more than four weeks.

In some ways it feels matter of fact, even an anti-climax. My husband is there in bed, he's been perilously ill, now he's regaining consciousness, and at some point he'll come home again. One part of my mind is reminding me that he's not out until he's out, and that this is only a small step forward. Simon is still in ICU, home to the

2% most critically ill of all hospital patients, with a nasogastric tube, a catheter and a tracheostomy (the latter with its 'cuff' down, which is why he can snore). However another part of my mind is saying that we've needed solid signs of hope for a long time and is encouraging me to feast on this as nourishment for the journey ahead. Either way, the feelings of joy and optimism well up from deep within and can't be suppressed.

Today, for the first time since this all began, I have no place here. Simon may be coming back to us, but for the moment all he wants to do is to catch up on lost sleep. I had been surprised to learn that being sedated doesn't count as rest in the usual sense of the word and therefore he is extremely sleep-deprived. Because he is lying quietly rather than thrashing about there are no pillows to plump or sheets to smooth, no wires to untangle, and no monitor to watch. Music no longer seems either necessary or appropriate. I am initially taken aback, even bewildered, to realize that my time is now my own again.

It's a good moment to catch up with family and close friends and to cautiously share the good news. Over a supper of spaghetti and red wine with Simon's brother Tim we dare to discuss life after St Thomas'. Tim cautions me to get my head around the fact that our adventure has hardly started and it may become harder and more complex from here on in. Simon will no longer be neutral and inanimate: there will be mood swings, frustration, perhaps even depression. How will he relate to me? He may have been going through physiological pain, but mine has been emotional. How will we square that circle? For the first time I find it hard to get to sleep, perhaps because of all these new considerations.

The following morning I arrive full of curiosity and excitement to find that Simon remains unreachable, but in a different way—he's still asleep! When he sleeps for most of the day I have to remind myself that this is the best possible thing, however tantalizing it is for me. He has a particularly lovely nurse who excels at the emotional intelligence dimension of nursing, making him comfortable, and when he wakes up, telling him where he is and getting him to respond to some simple yes/no questions. At one point Simon gives her—not me!—his first beautiful smile. One of our friends has written on the Facebook page about his special smile, which made me realise how I've taken that and so many other things for granted over the years.

In the half hour before I leave there are some delicious moments. Simon is lying stretched out full length on his back, eyes clear and limpid, hands behind his head, clearly listening along with me to the jazz singer Blossom Dearie. Then he sits up, not out of restlessness but to look around the ward. I show him the photos by his bed, and when I tell him that I have to leave now, he puts his first sentence together. The only word I can pick out is "cats", but who cares? A world of hope in a sentence!

Sunday is another quiet sleepy day, which is just fine by me. I am getting some much-needed space to catch my breath after feels like an extended emotional assault course. Simon is still silent but for the first time he shows interest in the whiteboard at the bottom of the bed and sits up unaided to gaze at it in a gentle and enquiring sort of way. I wonder if he can recognise any of the photos: of his bicycle, of him with the Dalai Lama, or collecting his doctorate. In the morning I had spoken of getting a springer spaniel, and in the afternoon he remarks, "The cats will have a new friend." It is an encouraging indication that his short-term memory is back in play.

Just before I leave, Simon suddenly announces, "I want to go to the cinema!" and makes a concerted effort to get out of bed. His identity as a film buff seems to have survived the coma. Unfortunately that thought seems to stay with him throughout the night, which is classified as agitated.

WEEK SIX
EXIT

CHAPTER 26

Wedding anniversary

On Bank Holiday Monday I arrive at the bedside to find Simon sitting up and reaching out to shake the hands of a cluster of doctors and nurses, as if he is hosting a business meeting. When they leave, we have our first proper exchange. "I've missed you so much!" I say. "Guess who I've missed." "The cats?" "Exactly!" Another knot of anxiety unties itself inside me—his personality is intact.

In the afternoon it begins to get really exciting. Nurse George tells Simon that he's been in St Thomas' for over four weeks. "Does my mother know?" comes the response. Simon correctly remembers his date of birth and the current year, although he thinks it's December rather than August. That's no problem, it feels like December to me as well. I ask what kind of music he would like to listen to: classical, jazz or world? "Amira!" comes the reply, in full confidence that I will have a CD to hand from our musician friend from Sarajevo. Fortunately I have three. I ask if there is anything else that he wants. "A pint of beer," comes the reply.

By the evening I am sitting alongside my husband rather than anxiously opposite him. Both physically and psychologically it is a massive turnaround. We are quietly hanging out together and it really feels that the nightmare is over and everything will be OK from now on. I read him the messages in the Get Well cards that have been piling up on the shelf and tell him who has visited. I can see he is trying to slowly digest this information although he soon gets tired and needs a nap.

The physiotherapists come by and join in the celebrations. "Extraordinary," they say, as Simon not only stands up, but walks virtually unsupported into the middle of the ward and back.

The other wonderful development is that Simon passes the 'blue dye test' and the 'swallow test'. These are examples of ICU 'low tech' which even I can understand. In the first test some blue food colouring is put into his mouth, and in the second test he is assisted in drinking a glass of water that has been coloured blue. After each stage the tracheostomy is suctioned to check that the muscles at the back of the mouth are functioning properly and that no blue dye has gone down into the lungs. Success means that for the first time in nearly five weeks Simon is allowed to have an ordinary drink. To my surprise I'm told that this can be anything he wants. I scuttle downstairs and return with some freshly squeezed orange juice from the AMT café. Although the nurse is expecting him to take a few tentative sips he drains the whole cupful in one go. "Extremely nice!" he comments. I cannot imagine how wonderful that orange juice must have tasted after 36 days of nothing but chemicals and mouthwash.

Tuesday morning finds me buying balloons. I am obsessed with the idea of tying them to the back of Simon's bed when we wheel him out of ICU, as if decorating a 'Just Married' car. (Fortunately I realise just in time how grossly insensitive this would be to the other families on the ward). But when I reach the bedside my heart drops. Simon has a new consultant and a kind but particularly anxious nurse and because he was agitated during the night he has been re-sedated. It's like a nightmare flashback: Simon is out for the count in his previous unnatural drug-fuelled state and the monitor is beeping away again above the bed. I then ask the nutritionist when the nasogastric tube will be removed, following the successful swallow test, and she replies that it won't happen until he's eating three proper meals a day. "That could be another week!" I exclaim. Another week in ICU—we could lose him yet. I pass the day in a mixture of anxiety and frustration.

Wednesday is our wedding anniversary, and to my delight and relief the consultant rota has unexpectedly changed again and we are back with Richard. This is where the consultant's familiarity with a patient can really make a difference. On the morning round Richard takes one look at Simon and asks for the sedation to be stopped and for both the tracheostomy and catheter to come out. Our nurse Janet also knows us well and when she hears that it's a special day she arranges for her and John the physiotherapist to take Simon down to the river in a wheelchair. The sun is filtering down onto the water through the giant plane trees, John and Simon are discussing their favourite beers, and I am trying to believe that this is really happening. "What a strange wedding anniversary," Richard observes, back on the ward. "Not at all: all the important things were in place," I reply.

"Thank you for looking after me: teamwork," Simon says to me that evening. It is unmistakeably his style, his personal way of expressing his feelings, and it is the best anniversary gift that I will ever have.

On my Thursday morning cycle ride into the hospital I stop to buy some bananas. Simon is sitting up in a chair beside the bed and eats one enthusiastically just as another new consultant arrives on her rounds. "This man looks far too well to be in intensive care," she says, before I can even ask her name. "What did he have for breakfast?" "Half a piece of toast—and a banana!" I respond. "Take his nasogastric tube out, then, and find him a bed somewhere else," she instructs Simon's nurse Jim.

Just before 1pm, Jim tells me that another bed has been found and departure is imminent. My face drops. My friend Lucy is coming up especially from Sussex for lunch—can the move be delayed? The answer is a reluctant yes, but only for an hour. The staff are willing to wait because the amount of clutter that we've accumulated around the bed will require at least two people to carry it all. I scuttle out for a quick but very good lunch washed down with a celebratory glass of champagne. As soon as I'm back on the ward our little cavalcade sets off. There are two porters pushing Simon in his bed and Jim and I bringing up the rear with his medicines and a ragtag of plastic carrier bags. We are waved out of the ward as if it was a royal procession. No balloons needed.

The lift goes up and up until we reach the very top floor of the main hospital block. We turn into Hillyers Ward and I glimpse a private room with an enormous glass picture window. Surely not? The answer is: yes! After over a month of dim shadows and artificial light we are led into a room suffused by brilliant sunlight. The window takes up an entire wall, and we are looking down on the glistening river Thames as it curves its way from Westminster Bridge to Tower Bridge and Canary Wharf. It is awesome, dazzling, extraordinary—one of the best views in London. Simon is the first to break the silence. "Happy ending," he says, and we both begin to cry.

CHAPTER 27

A room with a view

Simon is now subject to St Thomas' normal visiting hours: 2pm–8pm. I have to admit this is a relief for me after the total immersion experience of intensive care. I luxuriate in my first free morning for over a month, and relish going out and about on errands such as buying some respectable pyjamas and slippers for his convalescence.

Arriving on the ward just after 2pm is a rude awakening. Simon looks terrible. He hasn't slept at all, is consumed with anxiety, and claims to have had a fall in the night. In contrast to ICU, there isn't a nurse in sight. When I eventually find one she is adamant that there was no fall. This is our first experience of 'confabulation': a mind-bending mix of physiological and psychological factors in which Simon's brain, instead of functioning properly, appears to be making things up. In the circumstances, the nursing team agree that it's best if I can resume my all-day visiting routine. It's a disappointment to realise that my morning of freedom and fresh air was a one-off.

We are now back in the cash-strapped, under-staffed part of the NHS. The nurses are lovely but they're clearly stretched to the limit and have little time for anything more than supplying meals and medication and dealing with appointments and crises. What a contrast to the intensive care ward, a privileged realm in which nothing seemed too much trouble or expense and there was always a supportive medical team on hand. A doctor pops in briefly to see Simon on that first Friday and we then have no medical input of any sort until Monday afternoon, with the exception of one of the ICU nurses, despatched with typical 5-star thoughtfulness to check that we're OK.

When the door is closed our room has the quiet tranquillity of a remote cave high on a mountain, free from all the unnatural sounds of ICU. This tranquillity is rudely shattered on the first day when a pair of upbeat physiotherapists bounce in with an invitation for Simon to participate in a study of patients who have been on ventilation machines. Even for me they're speaking too fast to follow, and Simon's confusion levels rise exponentially. "We only came out of intensive care yesterday—give us a break!" I protest. Margaret, the senior of the pair, gets the message immediately. Over the coming weeks it proves a huge bonus for Simon to be involved in the study, and to get the extra attention and support that comes with it. However today it leaves me wondering how a fragile patient just out of ICU could possibly stay afloat without someone there to shield and support them.

When they have left Simon's habitual sense of hospitality comes back into play. "I must share this wonderful view with other people. We will invite someone different for lunch every day!" he proclaims. There is something very sweet and touching about such imperious beneficence, entirely oblivious to the rules and constraints of hospital life, and I don't want to cramp his style. "How about inviting someone to tea?" I venture. "Very well, we will invite my team!" Sure enough, on that very first day out of ICU six members of the St Ethelburga's team arrive for tea. The rule is that only two visitors are allowed at any one time, so I smuggle them across the corridor in pairs like a latter-day Noah. We keep the visit very brief, but that's all it needs to be—for them, the Ark is the reassurance of seeing their boss alive with his personality intact.

In an echo of home routines, we treat the weekend as down time and I begin to realise how exhausted I am. I'm functioning like a zombie. I requisition an abandoned armchair and footrest from a remote corridor of the ward and settle into a blissfully dozy and lazy couple of days in Simon's magnificent private room. The weekend is punctuated by visits from some of my own cautiously ecstatic core team: Philip and Mike, brother David, Tony and Denise. It makes a welcome change to be the quiet one while Simon is the centre of everyone's attention.

Simon doesn't have the concentration to read yet, so most of the time we just gaze out of the window together in contented silence, mesmerised by the silent fresco of the river landscape twelve floors below. He has seamlessly regained control of his mobile phone and is surprising family and friends with phone calls. From my side I'm enjoying the challenge of sourcing him the tastiest and most tempting of morsels from the hospital M&S, because one of our most pressing tasks is to get his appetite going again after so many weeks of liquid feed. "That was the best thing I've ever tasted!" he declares after eating an over-priced individually wrapped stick of mature cheddar. The room is perfumed with relief, and the scent is delicious.

The hospital systems whirr into action on Monday with a speed that suggests that Simon is likely to be discharged at the earliest opportunity. I can understand that he has made a sudden and miraculous recovery and that the bed will be needed for someone else, but it's still a shock to realise that very soon we will be out of here and largely abandoned to our own devices. I had welcomed the suggestion of ICU staff that Simon would probably need four weeks of supervised convalescence in St Thomas' because of the space it would give me for my own recovery and transition. I had it all planned: mornings catching up at work, afternoons at the hospital, and evenings unwinding in front of a box set of Downton Abbey. Instead, my frail husband is about to be returned to my care 24/7.

One of the reasons that the nurses on this ward are so busy is because of the vast but invisible task of arranging for their patients to get to all their specialist appointments in different zones of the hospital. In Simon's case, first he's seen by a general consultant, then by the neurologist, and then referred for another EEG and for hearing tests (it's becoming clear that hearing loss may be one of the biggest legacies of his illness.) Every outing from the ward demands a porter and one of the clunky wheelchairs that I'd first encountered in A&E. I'm not allowed to take him myself so if a porter shows up late the whole schedule of appointments collapses.

On the Wednesday, a mere seven days after leaving intensive care, Simon amazes Margaret the physiotherapist—and everyone else—by walking a full half mile along one of the hospital corridors. The weeks of delirious agitation have clearly kept him in shape, and it's a huge and very helpful boost to his confidence.

What comforts me most is to see how Simon is beginning to reclaim the richer depths of his mind and personality. A few days into his stay in Hillyers Ward he dreams that we are together with our cats in a huge old house with an orchard and that everything is peaceful and safe. It is a psychological turning point for him. Soon after, the ward consultant asks what his memory is like. "I've been wondering that myself," replies my husband. "Have you heard of the Hungarian film director Bela Tarr?" The consultant, like most of us, is not familiar with this august but relatively obscure Hungarian auteur. Simon continues, undeterred. "Well, during the night, I managed to remember every film he'd made and put them in chronological order." The consultant, who had probably been thinking of a simple question like "Can you name the Prime Minister?" beats a hasty retreat.

The film theme continues, not only because it's so close to Simon's heart but also because we have a tantalising aerial view of the National Film Theatre from his room. When Simon gets out of here, he decides, he will set up a film club. In November, free from the constraints of a working diary, he will have a bonanza at the London Film Festival. He recalls the year when he went to so many films in the Festival that he had to create a special spreadsheet to analyse the minimum cycling time between each venue.

Not everything is positive. One evening I rush in excitedly with the news that John Maver the Australian pianist is playing downstairs in the Central Hall. I get permission to take Simon down in a wheelchair only to find that all he can hear of Chopin and his adored Beethoven is a painful and discordant crash of chords. It's a sobering moment. Nevertheless the EEG results are fine and Simon is told that he will be discharged in two days time. To celebrate, he dictates his own message for the Facebook page—very, very, slowly—and we post some photos of him wearing a Moroccan gown instead of an invalid's pyjamas.

On the last evening, despite my misgivings, we organise a family breakout from the hospital so that Simon can collect his very own London Film Festival brochure from the NFT. We make a worthy addition to the parade of eccentrics to be seen on London's South Bank: Simon in a dressing gown, leaning heavily on a crutch, and me bringing up the rear with a hospital wheelchair that I have sneaked out of the building for the return journey. Clunk clunk clunk! I take a photo to celebrate this special moment, with Simon waving the brochure like a flag to mark the re-conquering of his physical, psychological and territorial freedoms.

In retrospect, the joy of these magical eight days suspended between earth and sky in Hillyers ward is something I will always treasure, particularly as it acted as a buffer zone between the drama and intensity of Simon's month in a coma and all the challenges to come. Learning to cope with the aftermath of his illness while being suddenly severed from the all-embracing love and care we had experienced at St Thomas' was to prove harder than I could ever have imagined. I had no inkling of how much I would miss the camaraderie and profound bonds that had been forged in ICU and how lonely and difficult the coming year was going to be.

AFTERMATH

CHAPTER 28

Mayhem

Simon declares that the autumn immediately following his illness is one of the happiest times of his life. As he explains it, he isn't in any physical pain (a rarity among convalescents) and has unprecedented leisure time in which to relish being alive as never before. The doctors, by contrast, are labelling his state of mind 'post-traumatic euphoria'. "There are things we can do about it, if it goes on too long," says his neurologist, in a chilling flashback to *One Flew Over the Cuckoo's Nest*. I resolve to keep our distance. From a Buddhist point of view, Simon's childlike joy and technicolour appreciation of everything he sees, hears, smells, tastes and touches is a natural consequence of coming back into circulation after a deep interior experience.

Only three things hold him back: his hands, his hearing and his head. Weeks of thrashing about in an ICU bed have damaged the ulnar nerves in his elbows so his hands are partially paralysed. What was previously a mild hearing problem is now much worse, probably as a side effect of the powerful antibiotics used to combat his pneumonia. He also experiences hearing distortion: for example, walking along the shore one day he hears the surf as church bells. In addition it's evident that his memory, his ability to concentrate and prioritise, and his emotional intelligence have all taken a hit.

The gradual re-booting of Simon's brain is an unfathomable process, during which our main source of professional support comes from an inspirational team of occupational therapists. As soon as mobility issues are resolved they move on to the 'higher level executive skills' that he will need to resume his job. However there's nothing high-tech about this process—instead, it's embedded into daily life situations. For example: to strengthen Simon's ability to multi-task, whenever we go out for a walk I am expected to simultaneously set him mental challenges such as listing all the countries that begin with an 'A'. The one time we try this, the breadth of Simon's general knowledge threatens to make me, not him, lose my footing.

It is also suggested that he strengthens his cognitive functions by helping out in the kitchen. On my birthday he triumphantly gives me a stack of the most complex cookery books he can find—Yotam Ottolenghi, never Jamie Oliver—and announces that he will cook me a recipe of my choice every day. I try to put a brave face on the ensuing chaos and expense.

While Simon flourishes, surrounded by people who encourage and support him, my situation is the exact opposite. In many ways this new phase is more difficult for me than the dramatic highs and lows of ICU. His precipitous discharge from St Thomas' eight days after coming out of intensive care has plunged me into the unfamiliar role of full-time carer. I struggle to manage a complex diary of outpatient appointments. I am expected to provide three nutritious meals each day, to build up his strength. There are also miscellaneous tasks such as hunting down shoes with Velcro fasteners, because with swollen hands Simon can't tie his own laces. I desperately miss the personal time for reflection and meditation that played such a critical role in sustaining me through the hospital vigil.

Life is further complicated by the fact that I've gone back to work on a half-time basis, partly because we're getting very low on cash. Some of my family think this is too soon. Other friends say the opposite: that it's important to nurture the other aspects of my personality so that I have an independent perspective to bring to our relationship. Although it's difficult to pick up the reins of running a small charity again, I quickly find out that my working environment is a welcome refuge from the non-stop demands of being a carer.

To cap it all, I can't sleep. The minute I lie down in bed beside

Simon all my senses seem to shift into high alert mode without any possibility of dozing off. My sister Kate points out that after weeks of watching over Simon's bed like a hawk this is hardly surprising. So each night I wait until he's gone to sleep and then creep downstairs to toss and turn on the sofa.

I take some comfort from the advice of my Buddhist teacher Lama Zopa that we can learn to enjoy problems just as much as we enjoy ice cream. The Tibetan Buddhist practice of thought transformation or *lojong* proposes that one of the most direct ways to develop positive qualities is through being rubbed up the wrong way. Just as wood is polished by sandpaper, the people who most irritate and provoke us are actually our most precious friends and allies because they provide a unique opportunity to develop qualities such as patience. Taken to its limits, *lojong* will eventually help us consider our problems not only helpful but even pleasurable and ultimately necessary for our happiness, at which point they effectively disappear. As Victor Frankl said: "When we are no longer able to change a situation, we are challenged to change ourselves."

In principle this makes complete sense to me but in practice, when every day is a non-stop torrent of demands and anxieties, I'm definitely being put to the test. Our first row occurs when we board a double-decker bus for an outpatient appointment. Simon is still unsteady on his feet and leaning on a crutch. "I'm sure someone will stand up for you," I say, glaring at the seated passengers. Both they and he ignore me; he insists on struggling up the stairs, and I feel angry and humiliated. In the local opticians he chooses the most expensive pair of glasses and lenses for himself, oblivious to our straitened means, while I stand by helpless and unwilling to contradict him in front of others. My new roles as secretary, treasurer and gatekeeper demand all the sensitivity and diplomacy I can muster. It's a delicate business, especially when the last thing I want to do is to impede the return of his independence and self-reliance.

Simon is charmingly unaware of the difficulties he leaves in his wake. One of the characteristics of a brain injury is that the person concerned is rarely aware of their limitations. A friend tells of a visit to a residential home where the encephalitis patients simply couldn't understand what they were doing there. Not only Simon but most of the people around us are equally unaware of our daily challenges and constraints, and since it doesn't seem appropriate to spell them out in public I become adept at picking up the pieces and covering for him.

"My religion is kindness," says the Dalai Lama. Buddhism proposes that the source of all true happiness and the very meaning of being alive are to do whatever we can to benefit others. When we reach our deathbed nothing else will matter. And since we are only one person, and others are numberless, what justification can there be for putting our own interests ahead of anyone else? I find this the most inspiring call to action in existence. As the Dalai Lama also says, showing kindness to others is not religious business but human being business, and the key to the survival of our race and planet.

The challenge is that we have to start somewhere, and one of the best places to start—although not necessarily the easiest—is through showing kindness to our nearest and dearest. This is what I'm now being called upon to do. Relentlessly.

I develop an intense admiration for the heroism of single parents who are able to put their own needs aside and without respite take sole responsibility for the welfare of another human being. Simon may not be a child, but like any parent I have the experience of never being off duty. What phone calls need to be made today? What clothes will he need? What mood is he in? Keys, phone and wallet are constantly misplaced. He loses his credit card five times, and repeatedly forgets the pin number. We come home from an afternoon out to find that he has left the front door wide open. I am constantly on my guard for all the things that can go wrong.

The chaos is compounded when a small, charming and untrained springer spaniel puppy called Lola joins the household. This is the liver-and-onion-coloured creature that Simon has longed for all his life, and which I promised to him in whispers when he was deep in his coma. Man and dog quickly become inseparable. Both the Ancient Greeks and the Celts believed that dogs have curative powers, and I watch as Lola gets Simon out of bed in the morning, as her feeding and walking routines help him regain a sense of responsibility, her antics make him laugh again, and her cuddling up calms him down last thing at night. Begrudgingly, I have to give her most of the credit for transforming him from a thin, frail and wobbly convalescent to a fit and energetic man who exudes good health. Better a springer spaniel than the black dog of depression, I tell myself.

CHAPTER 29

Loneliness

"Have you strangled him yet?!" Barbara is a former nurse, now a Buddhist nun, and it's the most helpful thing that anyone has said to me in weeks. Most conversations go "How is Simon?" and then in quick succession, "You must be so happy and relieved!" A smaller number of people will ask, "How are you?" usually because they've been through a comparable experience themselves. One friend writes: "I hope this finds you strong and happy". The honest response would have been, "No, actually, I'm feeling weak and miserable," but I don't have the desire or energy to type that into an email. It seems ironic that the times when we most need support are often when it's the hardest to ask for it.

Although I'm spending more time with my husband than ever before, I find myself unexpectedly lonely. Our experiences are proving to be so different, and he has lost the capacity to understand this. While Simon enjoys his new spaciousness, I am suffering from cabin fever. He feels liberated, and I feel enslaved. He wakes each morning full of energy and curiosity while I struggle with exhaustion. Simon tells me that he wants to give me tender loving care but the next moment gets completely distracted and is making extra demands on me instead. On Valentine's Day he memorises a beautiful and romantic poem in Hungarian but forgets to recite it to me and falls asleep before I come to bed.

As soon as our month of outpatient appointments is over we de-camp to our cottage in Devon. We purchased this some years earlier as an escape from London and a place to take our mothers on holiday. Interest rates were at an all-time low and the income from our London lodger covered most of the running costs. I feel extremely fortunate to have the option of a slower pace of life, fresh healthy food, and mile upon mile of beautiful country footpaths for Simon to explore as he regains his strength. I know that if he gets into any difficulties somebody will bring him safely home, in contrast to the hidden dangers of the Northern Line. Fortunately I can do most of my work at long distance, and once our new lifestyle has stabilised a bit I start commuting back to the office in London for three days each fortnight.

Most of our friends understandably conclude that we now need some private space. They probably imagine us enjoying an idyllic rural existence. They may also be assuming that we're cocooned by our families whereas that's actually not the case – they need their recovery time as much as we do. In London I could rely on the loyal support of friends such as my old college mate Sue, who crossed the city once a week bearing a home-cooked meal to share with us, but here I know almost nobody. As Stevie Smith would say, I'm not waving but drowning.

To my surprise, I'm also missing St Thomas': its routine and structures, its milling crowds and varied spaces, and most of all, the wonderful supportive nursing team in ICU. I calculate that the nurses will have cared for hundreds of other patients since we left, so I'm sure the attachment is one-sided. Nevertheless I still puzzle over the sudden severance of the profound bonds forged between human beings in their most intimate and vulnerable moments. It's like a love affair that ends with abrupt finality, to the bafflement of the emotions.

There are some advantages to being alone. I can see I'm not good company and I dread becoming a trauma bore. The intensity of our recent experiences continues to overshadow all my thoughts and conversation, drawing me back in like a magnet and dwarfing everything else. One of the bonuses of the hospital vigil was that it gave me licence to be completely candid. Life was raw and visceral, with ordinary convention stripped away. In contrast, I now find myself back in the subtle web and constraints of normal human discourse.

It's not exactly fun for anyone to listen to my problems, and Simon wants and needs a level of discretion about how his recovery is progressing. Some wounds are best licked in private.

When we do see friends, they invariably say "You're both looking so well!" It makes me glad for them, because it means they can take us off their worry list. However it closes the door to sharing how I really feel. And perhaps that's just as well, when most of the time my tears are ready to flow at the slightest encouragement. Instead, I spend any spare time in the company of my journal, which has perfect listening skills, doesn't censure me for being unable to move on, and never insists that I re-immerse myself in activities that are now of no interest to me.

When a colleague asks on the phone if I'm getting any 'me time', I find tears welling up. "In the very early hours of the morning," I think to myself, "and occasionally there's time for a bath." For the next few days this thought keeps popping up in my head and I watch how it catalyses resentment and self-pity. One of my Buddhist teachers famously advises that "less desire means less pain," and it is clear that the desire for 'me time' is simply making things worse. I drop the idea.

One of the challenges of wife-as-carer is the effect it has on the subtle configuration and calibration of a marital relationship. The independent feminist who signed up for a late marriage in which both parties pursued fulfilling careers and spent a few evenings each week together now finds herself joined to her husband at the hip. Not that he is exactly the same man that I married. One day I watch in shock as Simon, once the most gentle and patient of beings, angrily kicks a pile of DVDs across the room. His neurologist later admits that outbursts of anger are a common side effect of an anti-seizure medication called Keppra that he has prescribed for the coming year. "Some people get divorced because of it," he adds cheerfully. He had omitted to mention this to me. "For better, for worse," I find myself muttering under my breath.

I can never predict what any day will bring. Here's just one example, which I privately label 'post-encephalitis DIY'. Simon decides to patch up some missing carpet in our downstairs room, the kind of job he used to do with ease. He starts by taking our entire living space apart, repaints some wooden bookshelves and leaves them out overnight in the rain. Everything rests in confusion for a further week, at which point he orders a mitre saw to repair the skirting boards, but by mistake he gets it delivered to our London address. Meanwhile he paints the skirting boards and leaves them out in the rain, while forgetting for a second time to wear his painting overalls. He goes to London to collect the saw and on the return journey leaves it behind on the train. For the next month our living room looks like an abandoned squat. On Christmas Eve there is a Herculean tidy-up. Simon's mother arrives to a spotless house, can't see the problem, and upbraids me for complaining that her son is hard to live with. As a patient recovering from a life-threatening illness, Simon can do no wrong.

I come to the conclusion that however frazzled I feel inside, the most skilful response to all these challenges is to remain resolutely upbeat and un-flummoxed. I take an imaginary rosy-cheeked Devon farmer's wife as my model and gradually learn to go with the flow. We come up with a new nickname for Simon—'spanielbrain'—which serves as useful shorthand whenever things don't go to plan. Relaxed, amiable and good-humoured is proving far more important than tidy, organised or value for money, and my goal is simply to weather the chaos that each day brings and hope that our life won't always be like this.

Alongside the daily struggles, there are the golden moments of being alive together in this wonderful landscape, which suffuse me with joy. On a cloudless day we drive up onto Dartmoor, where the air is so clear that we can see the sea glistening on the horizon twenty miles to the south. Lola is running around in huge circles through the heather, ears flapping, and Simon is silhouetted against a dreamy blue sky. Another time we are down on the windswept beach, the puppy running across the sand like a streak in a post-Impressionist painting echoed by the larger streak that is my husband. Later that evening master and dog relax in front of the wood stove while we drink tea from china cups and saucers and download one of our favourite films to watch together.

Towards the end of a country walk when dusk is falling, I used to look in through cottage windows on scenes like this and wonder what it would be like to be safely on the inside. Except that I now know that nothing is safe. Will I ever forget what I've learned? I hope not. Some people have suggested that my continuing sense of anxiety is a sign of depression. Perhaps, but it is also a new realism: that nothing in the physical world is reliable or to be trusted, that the people who matter the most to us are deeply vulnerable, and that every situation can change in an instant. With a quick flick of the mind, I am back in that moment when Simon walked up to the house looking as if he was eighty years old, stumbling and incoherent, or when he was twisting and turning in agony in A&E. It's like opening the door to a locked-away room, which I quickly shut again.

CHAPTER 30

Gratitude

Exactly one year after Simon fell ill three things happen. He wakes one morning to find that his right hand has come fully back to life, he is fully discharged by St Thomas' as having made "a wonderful recovery", and we decide to throw a party.

We are now re-established in our London home. Simon has resumed his role as Director of St Ethelburga's Centre for Reconciliation and Peace on a half-time basis, and I am back working four days each week at the Foundation for Developing Compassion and Wisdom. One sunny Saturday morning a long-forgotten sound invades my consciousness—Simon playing arpeggios on the piano. He is celebrating the full recovery of his hand. Sensation has been building gradually over the past months: only recently, he triumphantly announced that for the first time he'd been able to turn the key in the front door. There's something about having the strength back in his right arm and hand that seems richly symbolic of his return to health. I want to dance, laugh and cry all at the same time.

The final visit to Simon's neurologist proves to be a milestone. Fortunately we've both taken the day off in some vague prescience of its emotional significance. It's an afternoon appointment, which gives me time to go out and buy some orchid plants to take as gifts. I get back to find that Simon has printed off photos of himself rowing on the estuary in Devon with Lola, bearing the title 'Simon Keyes. Suspected Encephalitis, ICU 1, 25th July – 1st September 2011.'

After seeing the neurologist we walk together along my old accustomed route up to the ICU ward. I discover that Simon doesn't know the way—and why should he? These corridors are full of my memories, not his. For the first time we press the buzzer together and arrive with our gifts at a reception desk full of new faces. I ask if any of the consultants we used to know are on duty today. "Richard is upstairs on ICU 2, why don't you go and find him?" In ICU 2 the young consultant is on the phone, so he asks the nurse to "find out what those people want." Meanwhile, other nurses come up to us grinning from ear to ear. "I can't believe it's you! You look so well!" they tell Simon. Richard joins the group: "Now I remember! The cyclist in Bed 12! The one with the picture of the Dalai Lama." "Thank you for coming back to visit," he says, "it's the best possible gift," before being called away to the latest emergency.

One dimension of our gratitude to the hospital and to the healthcare system that saved Simon's life is that the whole experience has been completely free of charge. I can't imagine how I would have coped with financial demands and decisions during that terrible first night in A&E, or have found the mental space and time to deal with insurance paperwork. I have friends in the USA who have taken years to pay off their debts from a routine operation, over and above their health insurance payments. On the other side of the Atlantic, Simon's illness would probably have bankrupted both ourselves and our families.

Everything needed for his treatment and recovery has been offered. This includes not only the visible medical care, but also the invisible, such as the blood tests sent away to specialist hospitals. There were also all the practical details that supported my visits to the hospital, from the flowers that welcomed and cheered me up on the front reception desk to the clean and warm toilets in the public areas. At its best, the NHS is an organism that functions like the barometer of a healthy society—a gesture of collective wisdom and mutual generosity which enables us to support each other through the worst of times.

"No one is as capable of gratitude as one who has emerged from the kingdom of night," wrote Elie Wiesel. I have my moments of gratitude fatigue, but most of the time gratitude flows effortlessly through me like a river in full spate. When something so powerful has happened to you, gratitude seems to take up permanent residence in one corner of the mind, perhaps as a defence and counterpoint against the brooding darkness, and the possibility of its recurrence. It's also the natural companion of our relief at a recovery so swift and complete that it has astounded even Simon's cool-headed medical team.

Buddhism, like science, teaches that the seeds of change are hard-wired into everything in nature. It's easy to deny such an inconvenient truth, especially when it applies to ourselves, so I also experience thankfulness for having been given a reality check that will accompany me through the rest of my life. On any day Simon could set off for work in the morning and come back half-dead. We part company after a drink in the pub (me on my bicycle, and him with Lola the spaniel) and five minutes later I wonder whether that ambulance weaving its way through the traffic is for him—or for any of our family and friends. The experiences we have shared make me acutely aware that we are fragile and transient creatures and that nothing material can be taken for granted.

There is a Tibetan Buddhist saying: "A day where you do not remember death is a day wasted". Waking up in the morning and believing, with at least half my mind, that this might be my last day on earth is like spicing up a dull dish. Reminding myself that external sources of pleasure and satisfaction are unreliable and time-limited helps me to re-direct my attention to inner pleasures, such as spotting an opportunity to make someone else's day a little bit easier or a little bit nicer. It's amazing how much genuine and unassailable satisfaction this can bring—and as dust turns to dust and ashes to ashes, it's all that will remain.

A year to the day after Simon fell ill we throw a party, both as a celebration and as a small gesture of gratitude to family and friends. Our social life has become so limited that many people haven't even seen him since he came out of hospital. The preparations are appropriately chaotic—for example, I'm not sure that Simon's invites are ever sent, and in the event no members of the family are able to join us. However we manage to gather together more than fifty guests for wine, food and live music in the beautiful and inspiring interior of St Ethelburga's in the City of London.

I often have difficulty knowing what to say at parties, but tonight there's no problem. For each person there is a thank-you: for a supportive email, an encouraging Facebook post, or a thoughtful gesture. I also enjoy the way that conversation is flowing between people from the different compartments of our lives, many of whom have never met each other before. I realise that it's not just a party to mark Simon's recovery but to celebrate how a community came together in a spirit of love and mutual support.

Simon has decided to make a short speech, and stands silhouetted against the stained glass window at the head of the nave, looking in better health than he ever did before. He holds nothing back, telling how even at his worst moments, pursued by demons in the darkest of places, he felt held in a web of love. "Perhaps this is what prayer is all about," he says. It's not your ordinary recovery speech, and the audience is mesmerised. "I'd like to thank all of you individually," he says, "but that isn't possible, so I've decided to thank just one person, on all our behalf."

I'd noticed that when our guests arrived he'd asked each one to write their name on a piece of paper, and now the basket of folded papers is brought forward. Our friend Wallee shuts his eyes and selects one to give to Simon. Simon reads it. There is a long silence, and then in front of everyone he begins to weep. I step forward to put a supportive arm around his shoulders and I read the piece of paper myself. I never wrote my name or placed a paper in the basket but the name on this paper is mine. I step back again: he has to handle this on his own. Many of the guests weep with him as he eloquently expresses his gratitude to me and I experience an explosion of feeling inside that takes all words away.

Back home in bed, I share the Bishop's observation that all the names in the basket could have been mine "because that's what any sensible person would have written." On the pillow beside me my husband pauses before he responds. "Actually, the Bishop is right. All the names were yours. I swapped the basket for another one which I'd prepared earlier." My first reaction is deep shock. At the moment when my name was drawn our dearest friends felt the universe had spoken—what a betrayal of their trust! My second reaction is pure joy. My smart, playful, free-spirited husband is back with us, and on full form. I start laughing uncontrollably.

"Now that you've recovered, I can begin to recover," I tell him. "From what?!" he asks.

Epilogue

Simon Keyes
January 22 2017

My last memory of the outside world is of sitting on a platform at Winchester Station having given what I thought was a careful briefing to my colleague. She says it was gobbledegook. How I got home I cannot recall – perhaps my memory had shut down by then or maybe pain or drugs erased it later. Still vivid though is the image of Alison and I the previous afternoon, dawdling with ice creams by the sunlit Thames after watching Ibsen's *The Emperor and the Galilean* at the National Theatre. I remember that, I didn't need to look it up.

The next physical sensation of which I was aware was an endlessly-repeating beeping sound, two different notes, the memory of which still fills me with dread. Then unfamiliar voices coming and going. A hammering on my neck. And a growing awareness of the beautiful presence of Alison, like a sun rising.

Between these two points I felt nothing. No pain, no movement, no world. But in my own private world of awareness I still existed. It was a terrible place. Here are two experiences that stay with me.

I am being pursued through a snowbound forest at night. My breath freezes in the air. I'm alone but I can sense a lurking presence – the only way I can describe it is like the crackling you hear beneath a high-tension power line – something inexplicably evil. Something dreadful has happened. I shout but I have no voice. I run into a house – a fire is burning but all the windows are open and there is snow on the floor. There's a row of orange anoraks on the wall but there's no-one here. I know I have killed them. I am trying to run away from something terrible I have done and I am being followed. I'm desperately cold, terrified, totally alone. Abandoned.

I find myself in a white room, everything ordered and impeccably clean. I float in mid-air. One wall appears translucent and I'm aware of dim shadows behind it. I hear the voice of my friend Philip saying, "You are in hospital, you are very ill, you are safe".

It is very hard to put these experiences into words. They read like dreams. No doubt there are psychological or, given that my body was awash with drugs, pharmacological explanations. But this was my reality. I can't say how long these experiences lasted, only that these places still exist somewhere in my mind. When I returned to consciousness I felt I had been away for a long time.

By Alison's account I returned to some degree of functionality in ICU but my memory of it is scrambled. Only when I moved to a ward upstairs did I begin to establish some bearings. In ICU I remember standing up and people looking at me. I remember being in a wheelchair talking about cycling with a doctor. I remember tubes being pulled out of my nose. I recall the taste of marmalade. I think I went to the cinema at some point. When I returned some months later to have a look at the ICU ward it was completely unfamiliar. I couldn't work out where Bed 12 was and I didn't recognise any of the staff.

Everyone seemed delighted by my improving condition but I found the first few days very difficult. I couldn't walk or hold my balance. My right hand didn't work and something had happened to my hearing.

Mentally I was all at sea. During the day when Alison was with me most of the time I felt safe. She told me what had happened and gradually I was able to piece together the story of this book. Between conversations I would sit contentedly watching boats on the Thames below. But once I was alone my mind ran riot, looping obsessively over random things. I couldn't stop rehearsing a list of the films of Béla Tárr. My recall of detail was extraordinary – I found I could name the cinematographers on Tárr's films something I didn't realise

I even knew. It was as if my memory had been reshuffled and long-hidden material suddenly exposed.

My emotions were alarmingly volatile. When two kindly volunteers came to visit all I could do was sob. They didn't return. I found I couldn't read. I could understand the words separately but couldn't connect them in my mind. One morning a priest arrived and invited me to read from the Bible. Laboriously I read each word as if there were a full stop after each one. They made no sense. Trying to watch a film was the same – each shot was disconnected from the next.

The worst thing was not being able to sleep. The room was very cold at night making the snowbound forest seem very close. My mind was a riot of violent thoughts and the terrifying sense of guilt I had experienced in the forest swept over me again. One night I gazed at a blue neon strip on the façade of a hotel opposite the hospital and experiencing such a depth of loneliness that I wanted to die. In the morning a nurse asked how I was but I couldn't find the words to explain and just cried. I found it hard to understand why no-one asked me about what was happening in my mind since for me this was a far more distressing problem than my physical condition.

To add to my confusion I was told that I was suffering from confabulation – false memories. I am sure, for instance, that one night I had a fall and another night had a conversation with a consultant, neither of which apparently happened. Those night terrors still linger in my mind, though, and for me they remain real.

I dreaded nightfall. And then on the fourth night after leaving ICU I finally fell into a deep sleep and found myself in a glorious dream. I had arrived at a beautiful old house on top of a hill, with an ancient orchard looking out over a landscape of trees and lakes and islands. Our two cats were stretched out in the sun. I had a small hovercraft and could flit around the countryside at will. I awoke with a feeling of radiance and knew that everything was going to be all right. From that moment everything was transformed and I experienced an euphoric feeling of life flowing back into my body which lasted many weeks.

I had arrived upstairs on a Thursday and, other than a quick check by a young doctor, I didn't receive any medical attention until the Monday. If I had felt abandoned since leaving ICU now the National Health Service delivered magnificently. Teams of doctors came to look at me and ordered batteries of tests – for brain, legs, ears, and hands. I got to see a top audiology consultant straight away. Various species of therapists waited on me, helping me stand up, testing my hands with playdough, fitting me with crutches (adjusting the slotted aluminium poles was quaintly called "cutting a stick"). I had fun falling off large balls onto the padded floor of a gym provided just for people like me. A man even came to cut my toenails and told me jokes which I enjoyed no end. A nurse offered to help me take my first shower for six weeks and when she didn't show up I managed to do it on my own. Clutching a bar of soap was beyond me and I fell over, joyfully wallowing around the shower trough in a fit of giggles.

One day a researcher called in and asked if I would consent to being part of a study she was conducting. I agreed and am very pleased I did so. Her tests, which included some curious magnetic shocks, mostly involved walking between orange cones laid out in a quiet hospital corridor. This provided me with a physical and mental challenge and after stumbling round the course for a few days I managed to "walk" half a kilometre without crutches. I felt Olympian.

After the dream I found I was able to begin to read again. There was a mountain of cards which I studied one by one over several days. I discovered that a Facebook page had been set up in my name. The knowledge that hundreds of people knew about my condition and had, in their own way, prayed for me was difficult to take in and I found I had to read the posts in small chunks to avoid being swamped with emotion. I was delighted to hear that some Buddhists in Singapore, whom I had never met, had bought live fish in a market and released them back into the sea in my honour. If my "forest" experience had been one of terrified abandonment, then the knowledge that I had not been spiritually alone was immensely comforting. I believe that all these good wishes may, in some mysterious way, have kept me alive.

There was one moment of real disappointment. Alison took me down to hear the hospital's resident pianist play. He asked what I would like to hear and I suggested the Chopin Ballade in A-flat, a favourite. He nodded and began to play. But all I could hear was an unrecognisable jumble of sound. It was a shock to realise that music, one of my great loves, might be lost to me in future. The audiologist speculated that the drugs which kept me alive may have caused permanent damage to the inner ear.

In all this I experienced no pain, just weakness. There was a regular flow of experts to my bedside who kept me busy with tests and exercises. Friends visited, and I enjoyed the camaraderie of other patients on the ward. I learned to eat again and when my appetite returned I found the taste of food intensely enjoyable. My sense of smell was particularly acute for several days. I realised I wouldn't be returning to work for some time and managed to dictate a list of outstanding tasks. More than anything, being with Alison was blissful, deepened by a growing awe as I gradually realised what she had done for me.

I was allowed to go home when I could demonstrate that I had mastered the art of climbing stairs with crutches. Being in my own bed, attended by two purring cats, was the safest place in the world. During the fine autumn days, Alison would take me to Kennington Park and leave me in the lovely café there. I would happily sit on the deck outside for several hours listening to the wind in the trees and watching the world go by, occasionally joined by friends.

Looking back, I can see that it was difficult for me to understand that I was still ill. I had no sense of the crisis I had been through and my euphoric mood masked my physical weakness and mental vulnerability. I was very difficult to live with. I kept losing things and leaving tasks incomplete. I was impulsive and could fly into fits of temper at the least provocation. One day I startled Alison by throwing a pile of CDs across the room, something I like to think was quite out of character. I was very slow to realise how tired and bruised Alison was after weeks of intense stress and putting the rest of her life on hold. Emotional intelligence was something I had to relearn. After a couple of weeks I was well enough to be left alone and she returned to work. I sensed in her a mixture of relief and regret.

Six months after the illness struck, I returned to work for one day a week accompanied by my occupational therapist who explained to my team what had happened to me. I soon demonstrated that I could perform as well as before and my interest in the work was rekindled. Somehow, though, I never really recovered my poise. Perhaps the organisation too had been bruised and got used to managing without me. I resigned and we left London to live in the countryside with Lola the spaniel. A few months later I was offered a professorship at a local university which has given me a wonderfully rewarding new career. I try to remember to thank Alison every day for saving my life.

Many people have described my recovery as "miraculous". Divine intervention? Who knows? There are certainly some strange things about it. I had been very severely ill and yet woke up relatively unscathed. Another encephalitis patient in St Thomas' at the same time as me who was unconscious for a much shorter time had to learn to speak again. The Encephalitis Society says starkly that "some loss of brain function is … a probable outcome of encephalitis". My long-term symptoms – concentration lapses, absent-mindedness, emotional volatility – are barely distinguishable from the general decline of middle age. The "euphoria" may have subsided but it has left in its place a new sense of joy in being alive. The way almost one hundred medical and care staff collaborated in saving my life and returning me to health is certainly a miracle of medical organisation and skill. The scale and warmth of the support Alison and I received from my family and friends, from colleagues far and wide, and even from strangers (the fish!) is extraordinary. I have seen so much of the essential goodness of people. All this is miraculous to me.

*   *   *

Five years later. I still have no recall of what happened during my time in ICU, but an unexpected thing has happened. In the last few weeks my hearing has begun to improve. Since the illness music has been an unpleasant blur which I have preferred to avoid. Now I find I am beginning to distinguish pitches again. At an event to mark the 60th anniversary of the Hungarian revolution I sit back with a smile, re-united with an old friend – the pounding rhythms and proud folk melodies of *Allegro Barbaro.*

"Without The Encephalitis Society I may not have survived"
Encephalitis is inflammation of the brain caused by infection or when a person's immune system goes wrong. Acquired brain injury, and in some cases death, are outcomes of the condition.
Encephalitis is a thief
It robs people of abilities that most of us take for granted; it can rob families of their loved ones and even in those families where the person affected survives, it often leaves them experiencing a complicated form of bereavement for the person they once knew.
The Encephalitis Society supports people in piecing their lives back together following Encephalitis. We also raise awareness of the condition and collaborate on research trying to recognise and treat the condition and its consequences more effectively.
Find out more
www.encephalitis.info
32 Castlegate, Malton, North Yorkshire, YO17 7DT, UK
Support +44 (0)1653 699599 - support@encephalitis.info
Admin +44 (0)1653 692583 - admin@encephalitis.info
The Encephalitis Society is the operating name of the Encephalitis Support Group.
Registered Charity Number: 1087843
Company registered in England and Wales Number: 4189027
Follow us on Social Media
@encephalitis
www.facebook.com/EncephalitisSociety
The Encephalitis Society
Support, Awareness & Research for Inflammation of the Brain

Afterword

Alison Murdoch has made a really important contribution with *Bed* 12. We need more literature around the impact of encephalitis on people and their family members. Alison's story provides this while also raising much-needed awareness of a condition which is more common than many other illnesses that receive more public and clinical attention: for example, motor neurone disease or certain forms of meningitis.

Narratives also have an active role to play in helping both the public and professionals understand the impact of this devastating neurological condition on those who survive it, on those who are family members and on those who are left bereaved. For people directly affected by encephalitis, such stories support their understanding, and help them make sense of what has happened. They can validate experiences and help reduce the sense of isolation and loneliness that individuals so often feel after unexpected trauma or illness.

Finally, narratives can prove to be a source of hope and inspiration, like this wonderful book, which is Alison and Simon's story. From experience I know how very valuable their contribution will be to those who sadly, but inevitably, will also experience encephalitis.

Dr Ava Easton, Chief Executive, The Encephalitis Society

Empty your mind of all thoughts.
Let your heart be at peace.
Watch the turmoil of beings,
but contemplate their return.

Each separate being in the universe
returns to the common source.
Returning to the source is serenity.

If you don't realise the source,
you stumble in confusion and sorrow.
When you realize where you come from,
you naturally become tolerant,
disinterested, amused,
kindhearted as a grandmother,
dignified as a king.
Immersed in the wonder of the Tao,
you can deal with whatever life brings you,
and when death comes, you are ready.

LAO TZU *TAO TE CHING*, CHAPTER 16,
ENGLISH VERSION BY STEPHEN MITCHELL

Because You Love Me

Your eyes are mirrors
of blessed reflections
because they watched me.

You have wisdom
you're the master of love,
when you caress me.

A thousand blessings
gentle madam,
because you watched me
because you have seen me.

Because you love so much,
I love you the most,
Because you love me,
you are the Woman,
you are the finest.

ADY ENDRE

(A Valentine's gift from Simon, 14th February 2012)

May Our Friendship Last Forever

May our friendship last forever;
May I sail upon your sea.
May we go through life together;
May there always be a 'we'.

May I be your endless sky;
May you breathe my gentle air.
May you never wonder why
Each time you look for me, I'm there.

May we be for each a smile
Like the warm, life-giving sun;
Yet when we're in pain awhile,
May our suffering be one.

May we share our special days,
The happiness of one for two;
And if we must go separate ways,
May my love remain with you.

NICHOLAS GORDON

(I came across this poem at a wedding service, and when
Simon was unconscious made a ritual of reading it aloud
in bed every night, before I went to sleep.)

Be present, O merciful God, and protect us through the silent hours of this night, so that we, who are wearied by the changes and chances of this fleeting world, may repose upon thy eternal changelessness; through Jesus Christ our Lord. Amen.

(from the Office of Compline; posted on the Facebook page by our friend Mhairi)

Watch, O Lord, With Those Who Wake

Watch, O Lord, with those who wake,
or watch, or weep tonight,
and give your angels charge over those who sleep.

Tend your sick ones, O Lord Christ.
Rest your weary ones.
Bless your dying ones.
Soothe your suffering ones.
Pity your afflicted ones.
Shield your joyous ones.
And for all your love's sake. Amen.

SAINT AUGUSTINE

We Cannot Measure How We Heal

We cannot measure how you heal
Or answer every sufferer's prayer;
Yet we believe your grace responds
Where faith and doubt unite to care.
Your hands, though bloodied on the cross,
Survive to hold and heal and warn,
To carry all through death to life
and cradle children yet unborn.

So some have come who need your help,
And some have come to make amends
As hands which shaped and saved the world
Are present in the touch of friends.
Lord, let your Spirit meet us here
To mend the body, mind and soul,
To disentangle peace from pain
And make your broken people whole.

JOHN BELL AND GRAHAM MAULE
(from *Love From Below*, Wild Goose Publications, 1989)

Closed Path

I thought that my voyage had come to its end
at the last limit of my power – that the path before me was closed,
that provisions were exhausted
and the time come to take shelter in a silent obscurity.
But I find that thy will knows no end in me.
And when old words die out on the tongue,
new melodies break forth from the heart;
and where the old tracks are lost,
new country is revealed with its wonders.

RABINDRANATH TAGORE

Dear God, Dear Barbican Poets, Dear Simon—

With all depth of emotion, with all the wonder of my heart, with all the intuition and language and instinct and questioning and celebration that comes from living on this planet – I pray, I dance, I shape a living poem in my body for you, Simon, for you, God, for you Barbican poets, for all who are connected to Simon's huge Beingness.

May my body in its intention be a prayer, one in which your spirit, Simon, is lifted and held in joy, in healing, in timekeeping of your own invention! In every blink of my eye I am affirming your life, Simon, and its spacious inclusion of so many myriad lives, my own included.

And last of all, I send – in this body-prayer-poem – the thing we cannot ever put into a jar, dissect under the microscope, diagnose, tweet, politically elect or extract in its original form from sacred texts: I send love – for that is what I feel for you, for the poets you gathered at the Barbican, and the police officers and troubled youths you gave me in Brixton, and for the world of people who love you and those who have yet to know your spectacular open arms.

In the Grace of the Known and the Unknown,

CHRISTINE HEMP, WASHINGTON, USA

(Christine previously led a poetry group that we attended, called the Barbican Poets, and participated in a poetry project that Simon designed for police officers and young people in Brixton, South London).

And finally . . .

The Germ

A mighty creature is the germ
Though smaller than the pachyderm.
His customary dwelling place
Is deep within the human race.
His childish pride he often pleases
By giving people strange diseases.
Do you, my poppet, feel infirm?
You probably contain a germ.

OGDEN NASH